OUR LADY IN OUR LIFE

Our Lady in Our Life

By
M. V. Bernadot, O. P.

Translated by
Mary Ryan

The Newman Press
Westminster, Maryland

1950

Nihil Obstat :
  JACOBUS P. BASTIBLE,
    Censor Deputatus.

Imprimatur :
  ✠ DANIEL,
    Episcopus Corcagiensis.

17 Novembris, 1948.

Second Printing, 1950

Manufactured by
Universal Lithographers, Inc.
Baltimore 2, Md.
U. S. A.

Contents

Our Lady Gives Us Jesus.

MARY stands at the well-springs of grace. Jesus Christ, God's gift to man, the source of our life, is Mary's gift also. Over and over in the incidents of the Gospel we are made to understand this law of love of the spiritual life: that Jesus gives Himself through Mary. Hardly had she conceived Him, than she hastened to carry Him to Elizabeth and John the Baptist; she presented Him to the Magi; she revealed Him at Cana. She shows Jesus everywhere. It is one of the most constant laws of grace. "They found the child with Mary His Mother" (Matt. ii, 11).

The Church understood this from the first. St. Bonaventure merely sums up Christian tradition when he writes that: "One never finds Christ but with and through Mary." He adds: "Whoever seeks Christ apart from Mary seeks Him in vain."

Mary's mission is to give us Jesus. She does it always. "Jesus Christ is the fruit of devotion to Mary," says St. Louis Mary Grignion de Montfort. "It is certain that Jesus Christ, for each man individually who possesses Him, is as truly the fruit of Mary's operation as He is for all men in general; so that if a Christian has Jesus Christ formed in his heart, he can boldly say: Praise and thanks to Mary; what I have is her effort and her fruit, and but for her I should not have it." [1]

---

[1] *True Devotion to Our Blessed Lady.*

In this little book we desire simply to show that Our Lady gives birth and life to Jesus within us; that it is she who gives us the spirit of Jesus; who makes us know Him in His mysteries and in His sacrifices, and who impels us to imitate Him. Through her we fulfil our Christian vocation: we receive the "adoption of children of God through Jesus Christ" (Eph. i, 5).

CHAPTER ONE

Our Lady Engenders Us to the Life of Grace.

I. Our Lady and Our Predestination.

II. Our Lady has Merited Grace for Us.

    1. The Annunciation.

    2. The Presentation.

    3. Calvary.

III. Our Lady is Our Mother.

IV. Our Lady is Mother of the Church.

V. "In Mary's Womb."

I. Our Lady and Our Predestination.

"Blessed be God, the Father of Our Lord Jesus Christ . . . who chose us in Him before the foundation of the world that we should be holy and unspotted in His sight in charity" (Eph. i, 3, 4).

So, from all eternity, God thought of us. He loved us. He chose and called us.

But to what does He call us? To be His children. In His love, He "predestinated us unto the adoption of children through Jesus Christ . . . unto the praise of the glory of His grace" (Eph. i, 5, 6). The incarnate Word is given to us as the model to be contemplated and reproduced:

"Whom He foreknew, He also predestinated to be made conformable to the image of His Son" (Rom. viii, 29). That is our supernatural vocation, to grow like Jesus.

But, in the thought of God, Jesus and Mary are inseparable. One cannot be like Him, without being like her. The same eternal act which predestined Jesus to be our Saviour and model predestined Mary to be intimately united with Him in the whole mystery of redemption, and consequently to be, along with Him, the exemplar of our life. When the Lord forms His elect, He considers them not only in His incarnate Word, but also in Her who is worthy to be called "mirror of justice," a pure reflection of His holiness: God wills us to become conformable to her image also.

Besides, she herself takes pains to impress that image on our soul. She is "the first agent of our redemption," says George of Venice: just as the chief royal agent inscribed the officers on the prince's lists and put the seal to his sovereign decrees, Mary inscribes in the "book of life" those who are predestined by eternal Love, and marks them with the seal of God. More than that, Blessed Hugh of Saint-Cher asserts that she is herself the "book of life" in which the Lord has written the names of the elect, in whom the Holy Ghost formed Christ and His members.

II. Our Lady has Merited Grace for Us.

Our predestination begins to be accomplished through baptism, which by giving us grace makes us partakers of the intimate life of God.   Baptism is our birth into the divine life.

Now this grace has been merited for us by Mary.

We must state clearly, first, that life comes to us from Jesus Christ, the one and only Saviour.   The sacrifice of the Cross is the only cause, the total, necessary, and sufficient cause of our salvation.   Not even the holiest of creatures could have redeemed us, whereas one drop of the blood of Jesus was enough to make superabundant atonement for our sins.   If Providence had so decreed, the incarnate Word would have offered His sacrifice without the coöperation of any creature: assuredly we should have been just as fully justified and sanctified, grace would have come down just as abundantly into our souls thus made children of God, and the stream of life would flow just as copiously.

But it pleased God to associate a Co-Redemptress with the Redeemer.   "As in Adam all die," says St. Paul, "so also in Christ all shall be made alive" (1 Cor. xv, 22). Eve, by her advice, had coöperated with the first man in our ruin: Mary by her consent coöperates with Christ in our salvation.   There is an admirable unity in the divine plan.   Woman contributes to our restoration as she had contributed to our fall.

We know well that the contribution of the new Eve adds nothing to the infinite riches of the sacrifice of the new Adam.   Yet, in the Christian tradition, we love to recall that if Our Lord is the principal cause of our salvation, Our

Lady is its secondary cause, and that the Mother has merited
for us, congruously and through love, what the Son merited for us on strict grounds of justice. Their merit is of
one order, since that of Mary depends entirely on that of
Jesus. Both are universal—unlimited in the Co-Redemptress as in the Redeemer.

Far from being an offense to Thee, Lord Jesus, this
teaching glorifies the superabundance of Thy redemption,
for from that alone the merit of Thy Mother draws all its
power. We believe Thy sacrifice to be so perfect, so rich
in grace, that it was able not only to save us, but to raise
up beside Thee a Co-Redemptress who along with Thee
could merit every grace for every man. Is not that the
fairest fruit of Thy precious Blood?

1. The Annunciation.

God, by a free decree of His wisdom, had from eternity
decided that the mystery of Christ would not be realized
without the consent of her who, by her free acceptance,
was to be "the helper of the new Adam." Mary entered
into that mystery as a coöperator, and truly merited grace
for us. Her answer to God's messenger: *Ecce ancilla Domini, fiat mihi secundum verbum tuum,* does indeed express
obedience, but still more it expresses resolution and authority. Until she has given her consent everything hangs
in suspense. The eternal counsels will depend for their
fulfilment on the "yes" that she can pronounce or withhold.

Once it is spoken, the new supernatural order begins. Her humble fiat is mighty, boundless; we may compare it to the fiat of creation. The one made us men, the other makes us members of the incarnate Word, sons by adoption of God.

That fiat of Mary's is the sovereign act of her life. It brings Our Lady into the accomplishment of the divine mysteries. From now on the mystery of the Incarnation cannot unfold itself without her: through her, God is about to accomplish His great mystery, the mystery which redounds "unto the praise of the glory of His grace" (Eph. i, 6), the mystery of Christ, namely, Christ in us. When God decides to give Himself to creatures, He will do it through Mary, the intermediary between us and the divine life. The operations of union, of love, the diffusion of grace, will be performed by God through Mary.

Mary knew it. A prophetic light showed her the whole mystery of her Son, and she surrendered herself to it unreservedly. "She knows, she feels, she sees to what God is drawing, calling, raising her, and she enters into this divine state full of grace, of light, and of desire to serve God in this high ministry." [1]

No doubt she did not know from that first moment the particular happenings, the secondary circumstances of the life of her Son, but she clearly saw what was essential in

---

[1] Cardinal Pierre de Bérulle, *Vie de Jésus,* ch. xv.

it, its principle and its goal. She knew, through the angel's words, not only that He was the "Son of the Most High," and that she would have the glory of being Mother of God; but that she would call Him "Jesus," that is Saviour, and that she would have to give Him for the salvation of men. The great design of God, the diffusion of divine life through her Son, was apparent to her.

Can we doubt it? The whole of tradition asserts it. Our Lady assiduously read the Scriptures, the deep things of which the Holy Spirit revealed to her. She could not but know the great design so often announced by the prophets: the mysterious nuptials that the Lord intended to contract with human nature: "I have loved thee with an everlasting love," so He spoke through the prophet Jeremias (xxxi, 3); "therefore have I drawn thee taking pity on thee." And through Osee (ii, 19): "I will espouse thee to Me in justice and judgment; and in mercy and in commiserations. And I will espouse thee to Me in faith."

Our Lady penetrated the deep sense of these texts and of many others, and she knew that the Messiah, her Son, would be the bridegroom of that mysterious marriage foretold in the Canticle. In her heart she already loved with the same love her Son and those with whom He was to be so closely united. If St. Paul, not long after, recognized so clearly that mystery of the union of Christ with His members, how brilliantly clear it must have been in the mind of Our Lady, who was to play such a decisive part

in it! She saw, and she saw in an incomparably more perfect light, that her Son would be the Head of an immense
body, and that the mystery of the Incarnation would not
be completed in one instant in her womb, but would be
accomplished little by little until the end of time by the
formation of Christ's members.

She understood that as she was called to be the Mother
of the Word incarnate, she must conceive Him in His
totality, as St. Augustine was to express it, in the Head and
in the members; and that her maternity would not reach
its full perfection until she brought forth the whole Christ.

It was to the whole of this mystery that the Archangel,
speaking for God, asked her consent, and Our Lady willed
the whole of this mystery. At the same time that she accepted the motherhood of Jesus, she accepted the motherhood of the members of Jesus: from that day she was our
mother. "My sweet Son Jesus is not *unigenitus,* an only
Son," said Mary to St. Gertrude; "but *primogenitus,* my
first-born Son, because I conceived Him first in my womb;
but after Him, or rather through Him, I conceived you all
by adopting you into the innermost core of my mother-
heart, so that you might be at once my children and His
brothers." [2]

"In the womb of His most pure mother Jesus Christ
not only took mortal flesh, He also took a spiritual body,
formed of all those who would believe in Him. So that

---

[2] St. Gertrude, *The Herald of Divine Love,* Book IV, ch. iii.

it can be said that Mary, bearing the Saviour in her womb, bore also all those whose life was included in His. Therefore, all of us, inasmuch as we are incorporated into Christ, are born of Mary's womb like the body united to the head . . . In a spiritual and mystical but real way we are called children of Mary and she is the mother of us all." [3]

2. The Presentation.

The heavenly Father had given Jesus to Mary. "Every child belongs to his mother, but no child in the same degree as Jesus to Mary, for she is unique in having conceived, formed, and brought forth her Son alone, with no human coöperation of any kind."[4] Jesus is her treasure, and she has all the right of a mother over Him.

But now the Lord reminded her by an inner light that she must give up her treasure, and that Jesus, the fruit of her womb and the supreme possession of her life, must become the possession of all, a common good, dedicated to the salvation of the world.

It was that sacrifice of her rights that the divine Mother accomplished when she presented her Son Jesus in the Temple. To submit humbly to the Law, to surrender her own self, was nothing more than the course of her everyday life. But now something much greater was asked of her: the sacrifice of her Son. Simeon was there to remind

---

[3] Pius X, *Ad diem illum,* Feb. 2nd, 1904.
[4] Msgr. C. L. Gay, *Conférence XXXV.*

her of the great mystery of the Redemption: her Son was the Saviour and the Redeemer, He was to die for His brethren. Our Lady was to hand Him over to sacrifice, to death. She did it unhesitatingly, unreservedly, definitively. She abandoned her Son to the absolute rights of divine justice for the salvation of men; she gave Him to be a victim. And she offered herself to go with Him wherever it should please Him to call her.

"They reach the altar," says St. Thomas of Villanova; [5] "the Virgin falls on her knees, burning with more fervent love than the seraphim in heaven. She has her Child in her arms; she offers Him to God as a sacrifice of most acceptable odour, with the prayer:

"O Almighty Father, accept the oblation that I Thy servant make to Thee for the whole universe. Take this Son who is ours: mine in time, Thine from all eternity. I give Thee boundless thanks for having raised me to the dignity of mother of Him whose Father Thou Thyself art. Take this most holy Victim from the hands of Thy servant. This is the morning sacrifice which will one day on the arms of the Cross be the evening sacrifice. Good Father, look favorably on my offering, and consider for whom I am offering it to Thee."

It is true, Mary took her Son back with her to Nazareth;

---

[5] *Sermon on the Purification of the Blessed Virgin Mary.*

she lived with Him in the sweet intimacy of family life. But we may be quite sure that the memory of Simeon's prophecy never left her, that she lived in the thought of Jesus' sacrifice, in the prospect of Calvary. The holy old man had held up the cross before her: her eyes were ever fixed on it. With all a mother's love, she busied herself about the divine Child and the adolescent, but she was as a priest preparing the victim for immolation. Like Abraham climbing up the mountain on which he was to immolate his son, Mary each day made one step more towards Calvary.

Thus, on the day of the Presentation, she renewed her acceptance of the great mystery, consenting to sacrifice her Son for our salvation. It was because of us that she suffered.

3. CALVARY.

Enlightened by a prophetic light, John the Baptist recognized in Jesus the Redeemer, Him who would die to expiate the sins of men: "Behold the Lamb of God," he said, "behold Him who taketh away the sins of the world" (John i, 29). How much more brilliantly clear that truth was in the eyes of Our Lady! Her perfect understanding of the divine Scriptures would have sufficed to reveal to her the fearful Passion towards which her Son was journeying. Did she not read in Isaias this clear prophecy: "There is no beauty in him nor comeliness; and we have seen him and there was no sightliness, that we should be desirous of him; despised and the most abject of men, a man of sorrows and acquainted with infirmity; and his look was as it were hidden and despised, wherupon we esteemed him not" (Isaias liii, 2, 3)?

Mary read and meditated on these and other prophecies; she knew that they would be fulfilled in her Son. Doubtless Jesus Himself often spoke of them with her as of the great work they had to accomplish in common. If He willed several times to announce to His disciples His Passion and death at Jerusalem, how could He have been silent about them to His mother, who was to have so important a share in them? He spoke of these things to her so that she might live with Him in the thought of the sacrifice, and that she might say like Him: "I have a baptism wherewith I am to be baptized" (Luke xii, 50).

Can we imagine what the thought of that terrible Passion meant to Our Lady, and the presentiment of the cross that ever stood before the eye of her mind? Think of the agony of any other mother knowing beforehand the tortures that her child will have to endure; and you will suspect something of Mary's inner martydrom as she read in the Scriptures verses like: "He was wounded for our iniquities, he was bruised for our sins . . . He shall be led as a sheep to the slaughter . . . and he shall not open his mouth . . . The Lord was pleased to bruise him in infirmity . . . He was reputed with the wicked . . ." (Isaias liii, 5-12).

Blessed Angela of Foligno said of Jesus: "He abode in sorrow." The same might be said quite exactly of Our Lady, who felt each year, each day, that she was drawing nearer to the dreadful hour in which her Son would be handed over to the uttermost malice of men.

Now, it was for us that from the first she accepted that martyrdom. The same prophecy that revealed to her the depth of the sufferings of her Son spoke to her also of their purpose, the salvation of men:

"Surely he hath borne our infirmities and carried our sorrows . . . The chastisement of our peace was upon him and by his bruises we are healed . . . If he shall lay down his life for sin, he shall see a long lived seed" (Isaias lxiii, 4, 5, 10).

Our Lady entered into God's designs, and accepted beforehand the sacrifice that would become a gushing fount of life. Although her heart was pierced, she longed, like Jesus, for the hour which was to give a "long-lived seed" to her Son and to herself, and restore to God His lost children.

When that formidable hour had come, Mary was ready, and she stood erect by her Son's side: "Now there stood by the cross of Jesus his mother" (John xix, 25).

"She stood," and like a sacrificing priest, she offered her victim freely, voluntarily. No creature can have any idea of her pain in those terrible hours, a pain made extreme by the ineffable tenderness of her heart, by the very

fineness of her physical constitution, and, above all, by
her spiritual insight; for she was both a mother and bound
to her Son by a unique privilege of perfection and of holiness.   And yet we must not think of her as overcome, faint-
ing, supported by the holy women. No, *stabat,* she "stood,"
like the priest at the altar, absolute mistress of her thoughts,
her feelings, and her will.   She did more than submit to
the demands of divine justice, she entered unreservedly into
the designs of the eternal Father, sacrificing her only Son
for the salvation of the world. "She had to unite with the
eternal Father and they had in common to deliver up to
execution Him who was their Son in common, for that is
why Providence called her to the foot of the cross." [6] She
was implementing the consent spoken at the Annunciation,
confirmed at the Presentation, renewed all her life long:
she was giving her Son for us.

The dominant thought in her soul was the thought of
our redemption. "When with her mother's eyes she looked
fixedly at her Son's wounds," says St. Ambrose, "what was
uppermost in her mind was not her beloved Son's death
but the salvation of the world." [7]   If she could have taken
Jesus down from the Cross and saved Him from death she
would not have done it, any more than Jesus Himself willed
to save Himself from His executioners. She, too, said in

---

[6] Bossuet, *Sermon I on the Compassion.*
[7] St. Ambrose, *Expositio Evangelii secundum Lucam,* Book X, no. 1532.
J.-P. Migne, *Patrologia Latina,* XV, 1837.

her heart: "The chalice which My Father hath given Me, shall I not drink it?" (John xviii,1 1). If all her life she was intimately united to her Son, willing all that He willed, never was that union more complete than in the hour in which Christ consummated His mission. "The will of Christ and that of Mary formed but one, their two holocausts formed but one. Jesus and Mary offered their sacrifice similarly to God: Jesus in the blood of His body, Mary in the blood of her heart." [8]

That is why Our Lady stood at the foot of the cross, in the attitude of a priest, immolating her Son to give us life.

At the same time she offered herself, with her heart crushed and her soul in desolation, with her grief, "more vast than the sea" (Ecclesiasticus, xxiv, 39).

III. Our Lady is Our Mother.

We have shown that Mary twice became a mother. The first time at Bethlehem, in the expressible sweetness of supreme joy, the Word incarnate came into this world. The second time, on Calvary amidst indescribable anguish, a whole people came to the life divine. A mother is she from whom we have received life: I am born to grace through Our Lady: she is therefore truly my mother. I must not understand that name in a figurative sense, but in the most literal and real sense. Through a woman I received the life of the body, Mary has given me the life of

---

[8] Arnoldus Bonneval.

the soul, the life that unites my soul to God. She has loved me and suffered for me. Her heart, a heart over-flowing with life, a woman's heart, a mother's heart, pours out its love on me. She is a perfect mother, possessing in its fulness and able to give out to me the divine life by which I must live. Her motherhood is in the image of God's fatherhood. She gives me everything with utter devotedness and affection. Since God has given her the office of distributing all His gifts to us, he has also charged her to do it with His love. That is her mission. It is not her function to teach, or to judge; she loves, she is a mother.

She is so much a mother that wherever I see her exercising her divine maternity towards Jesus, I see her also exercising her maternity of grace towards us. At the crib she holds Jesus in her arms and presents Him to the shepherds and the Magi; in the Temple she offers Him, but it is for us; on Calvary she keeps watch by her Son and immolates Him for our salvation. It is at the moment that she is fulfilling her last maternal duty towards Jesus, that He announces her motherhood of souls.

IV. Our Lady is Mother of the Church.

The power of her motherhood extends to the whole Church. Her mission was but beginning when she gave to Christ His material body: now she gives Him His spiritual body. From her body was formed the body of the Person of Christ. From her love, her active affection, is formed

His Mystical Body: Jesus is only the first of her sons. She is, like Eve, "the mother of all the living" (Gen. iii, 20). She seeks out the predestined to incorporate them into Christ. All who are predestined to grace are predestined to be her children.

She works to bring about the unity of souls in the Mystical Body. That is the work of her maternity. Through her is formed each mystical member of Jesus and in her all are united organically to the Head.

It was for the sake of the Church that Mary remained on earth after the Ascension; she performed for it the office she had already performed for Jesus: she watched over its cradle. The Scriptures have preserved for us the earliest vision of the Church: in one spirit, in prayer, the brethren of Jesus gathered about His mother. They needed her in order to preserve the spirit of Jesus and not to flinch when persecution began. The dangers that had beset the new-born Child of Bethlehem now beset His Mystical Body. The Mother who saved the Christ Child had to be there to watch over the nascent Church. Is it not a striking thing that the mystery of Christ which could not begin at the Incarnation except through Mary, entered into its plenitude on the day of Pentecost, again through the mediation of Mary?

We invoke her every day by the title "Ark of the Covenant." The Ark of the Covenant in the Old Testament sheltered, in the silence of the Holy of Holies, the whole treasure of the faithful people, was their protection and their hope.   Our Lady, acting always hiddenly, is at the well-spring of the life of the Church.   As mothers do, she hides in the privacy of the home; but she distributes life. She is the Ark of the Covenant of the Church, its secret strength, the heart of its holiness.

V.   "In Mary's Womb."

Over and over again St. Paul explained to the early Christians that we live in Christ: *in Christo Jesu*. We are incorporated in Christ, bathed in Christ, clothed with Christ. Christ is the vital source of that supernatural life by which the members of His Mystical Body live. But just as Christ's human life was first brought into being in Mary's sacred womb, so our supernatural life is formed and brought into being through the agency and beneath the shadow and protection of the same Sacred Mother.   So that we may say that we live, as it were, in Mary's womb.   Is not Our Lady's maternal power also a sort of atmosphere in which Christendom lives?   All the elect are formed in her spiritual womb.   The life of grace is not, in its first beginnings, a perfect life; it has its movements of growth, it has its childhood; it is a life in process of formation.   It needs a mother for the period of its weakness.   And this period of childhood lasts the whole of our life on earth.   As long as we are here we are in the period of childbirth, of formation. Even the saints are children in this respect.   And see what intimacy with Our Lady comes of that, since we are being formed, as it were, in her womb. As long as the child lives in its mother's womb, it is one with her, it is dependent for the continuance of its life upon her. So all our life long Our Lady carries us in the warmth of her love. She feeds us with the grace of which she has the fulness.

Is there any fervent Catholic who does not feel that he is living and growing in the atmosphere of a mother's love? "The Queen of grace and of mercy bent over her sons and daughters," Blessed Angela of Foligno tells us. "She bent down and blessed them with a vast blessing, and drawing them to her heart she embraced them unequally. It seemed as if her arms were the outstretched arms of love. She was entirely luminous and seemed to gather them into herself in endless light. Do not imagine that I saw her arms of flesh: she was wholly light, admirable light. The Blessed Virgin pressed her children to her heart, and by virtue of the love that flowed from her inmost being, absorbed them into herself." [9]

[9] Blessed Angela of Foligno, *Visions et Révélations,* ch. xlviii, Edit. Hello.

CHAPTER TWO

Our Lady and the Growth of Our Life.

I. Our Life Must Grow.

II. Our Lady the Prime Minister of Grace.

III. How?

    1. Our Lady intercedes for us:

        (a) Her prayer is enlightened.

        (b) It is the prayer of a mother.

        (c) It is all-powerful.

    2. Our Lady acts upon us.

IV. The Presence of Our Lady in Our Life.

I. Our Life Must Grow.

All life tends to grow and expand: the child's law is to become a man. So of supernatural life: it must develop. God might have decided that like the angels, we were to settle our eternity by one single act of the will; instead He willed that we were to have the power of growing, and He gave us the time and the means. The grace that we get in baptism is a starting-point. "The path of the just," says Holy Scripture, "as a shining light, goeth forwards and increaseth even to perfect day" (Prov. iv, 18). St. Paul often recurred to this truth, and he tells us in every

mood and tense how we must grow in grace "unto a perfect man, unto the measure of the age of the fulness of
Christ" (Eph. iv, 13).

Our Lady helps us to grow in Christ. She is a mother.
A mother is not satisfied with giving birth to her child:
she watches over its growth, desires to bring it to perfection. Our supernatural growth requires at every moment
some fresh exercise of energy, but this demands actual
graces, without which we should at once come to a stand-
still. Through Our Lady come these graces, all the graces
that we need, for all the details of our life, for all our
difficulties, for every step in our progress.

Pentecost is an image of what will take place until the
end of time. On that day, the Holy Spirit fulfilled God's
eternal plan and came down upon the faithful at Mary's
prayer: it will be so always. "Our Lady," says St. Bernardine
of Siena, "has received a sort of jurisdiction, I might say
a sort of authority over all the communications of the Holy
Spirit."

No doubt the distribution of grace belongs by His own
right to the sole Mediator, Christ. God alone can produce
grace in the depths of the soul. Only the divinity can give
divine life, says St. Thomas.[1] But God has willed that because of their intimate union in the Redemption Christ and
His mother should also be united in this distribution of

---

[1] St. Thomas, *Summa Theologica,* IIa, IIae, q. 112, a. 1.

grace. God might have given it out alone: He pleases to distribute it through Mary.

II. Our Lady the Prime Minister of Grace.

Everything that the Passion of Christ has merited for us in rigorous justice, Mary's Compassion has co-merited for us, not indeed in justice but in virtue of her unique association with the meriting Christ. Today, Our Lady distributes to us graces thus merited in her intense suffering. "Having lent her ministry to the work of the redemption of men, in a parallel way she exercises the same ministry in dispensing the grace which perpetually flows from the cross, endowed as she is for this purpose with almost unlimited power." [2]

Christ has associated her closely at every stage with His mystery. The Incarnation could not take place without her free consent, "so necessary was it for men that Mary should desire their salvation." [3] On Calvary she suffered with her Son for our salvation. Is it not congruous that she now dispenses the effects of those mysteries, the graces of sanctification? "Since God willed to give us Jesus Christ through the Blessed Virgin, this order remains unchanged. The gifts of God are without repentance (Rom. xi, 29). It is true and will always be true that having once received through her the universal principle of grace, we still receive through her ministry its various applications in all the dif-

---

[2] Leo XIII, Encyclical, *Adjutricem populi,* 5 Sept. 1893.
[3] Bossuet.

ferent states that make up the Christian life. Since maternal
love contributed so greatly to our salvation in the mystery
of the Incarnation, it will have a share eternally in all the
other operations which depend on the Incarnation." [4]

Today in heaven Christ applies to us the merits of His
sufferings; He is our advocate, ever making intercession
for us, says St. Paul (Heb., vii, 25). And so with Mary:
on earth she saved us as co-redemptress; in heaven she is
our advocate; ceaselessly she pleads for us. She asks that
all the graces merited by her Son and by herself be applied
to us. She holds in the mystery of sanctification a place
similar to that which she occupied in the mystery of the
Incarnation and Redemption.

St. Paul writes thus of Christ: "He is always living to
make intercession for us, for it was fitting that we should
have such a High Priest . . . We have such a High Priest,
who is set on the right hand of the throne of majesty in
the heavens . . . He hath obtained a better ministry, by how
much also He is a mediator of a better testament . . ." (Heb.
vii, 25, 26; viii, 1, 6). We may in due proportion apply
these great texts to Our Lady. She sits at the right hand of
God to intercede for us, to exercise her ministry of mediation which is literally priestly. She is the minister of grace.[5]
Her divine maternity has conferred on her a priesthood,
which she exercises along with that of her Son of which

---

[4] Bossuet, *Third Sermon for the Feast of the Conception.*
[5] Pius X, *Princeps gratiarum largiendarum ministra.*

it is the complement.   She is a virgin priest, the helper
of the eternal priest, the universal mediatrix, who will distribute throughout eternity the divine life to God's redeemed
ones.

For Mary is a mother, with all the qualities of a mother.
She has given us birth at the price of immense suffering.
It was not with the intention of abandoning us.   She wills
to perform all the functions of a mother: to feed, develop,
increase the life of her children, to make them members
of Jesus. The whole of salvation comes to us through her.
"When Jesus on the Cross said to John and in his person
to the whole Church: Behold thy mother, he set Mary up
as administrator of the whole Church.   As if He had said:
no one can be saved except through the merit of My cross
and My death; and no one can have a share in My blood
except through My mother's intercession.   Only he who
has Mary for his mother shall be the son of My sufferings.
My wounds are eternal springs of grace always flowing,
but they shall only pass through Mary as channel.   He
who does not love Mary as his mother, will invoke the
Father in vain . . ." [6]

III. How?

1. OUR LADY INTERCEDES FOR US.

Our filial love feels a legitimate satisfaction when it can

---

[6] Vincent Contenson, *Theologia Mentis et Cordis,* Vol. III, p. 210. Ed.
Vivès.

get some understanding of the way in which our Mother distributes the divine life: Mary intercedes for us, and she acts on us.

(a) Her prayer is enlightened.

The elect in heaven know, in the vision of the Word, everything that can interest them on earth, in proportion to the mission they fulfilled in the world. The perfection of their happiness demands this. Fathers and mothers know the vocation, the dangers, and the needs of their children; they can come to their aid. It is a present knowledge the perfection of which depends on the degree of their bliss.

Our Lady has perfect knowledge of what concerns the redeemed, her children. Could she exercise a real maternity without precise knowledge of our vocation and our needs? She must be wholly at the service of all and of each. She reads our souls by her prodigious maternal intuition. She sees us in the Word of God. She knows us as God knows us. She sees us all individually, as the good Shepherd knows by name each of His sheep. Let no one be surprised when we say that her knowledge is proportioned to eternity. She knows my personal vocation, God's thought about me, the perfection that I must realize, the glory that I must attain.

She knows also my history, my lapses, my present dangers and the graces that I need, in order to persevere. Because she is associated with the work of our sanctification, God reveals to her His thought in regard of all the redeemed. Their salvation is of deep concern to her, as to a mother: they are the children of her sufferings. Her bliss would lack much if she could not watch over the supernatural life of her children. The perfection of her union with God gives her a very perfect knowledge of our love, our desires, our infirmities, even of needs that are hidden from our own eyes. Do not earthly mothers read into their children? She knows thoroughly, and can help me realize, the secret of my personal vocation which I am ignorant of.

How blessed it is to think that Our Lady often prays for us in needs that we do not know of! One of our misfortunes is that we are blind about ourselves. But a mother's eyes see into everything. Mary sees everything in the divine vision. Often, without being invoked, she intercedes for us, moved by our unrealized wretchedness.

"To Thee, Mother of mercy, mother of the wretched, the exiled children of Eve cry out. Our very miseries cry to thee. Our wretchedness has its clamorous voice. This valley of the world echoes with weeping, so that if men do not call on thee, our very wretchedness itself cries out to thee. It cannot be silent before thee and thou canst not but hear it because thou art the Mother of mercy." [7]

(b) It is the prayer of a mother.

Above everything else, Mary loves us.

God is love. Christ saved us through love: "He loved

---

[7] Richard of St. Victor, *Explicatio in Cantica Canticorum,* J.-P. Migne, *Patrologia Latina,* CXCVI, 475.

me and delivered Himself for me" (Gal. ii, 20). So, too, Mary. She was swept along in the movement of infinite love, and her maternal affection led her to offer her Son for us.

Need we insist on this? If there is any reality to which the faithful have ever been fundamentally attached, it is that of the ineffable affection of Mary for men. She loves us as a mother, a mother who has suffered much: we are her children and have cost her an unspeakable martyrdom.

She loves us with a genuine love. She wants to deliver us from our evils, our miseries, to take us out of our shame, to lift us up as a mother does, to draw us to God, to fill us with life. If there is one amongst her children who is weak and little, to him she hastens, for him her pity is moved and her affection is most active.

It is always Jesus that she loves in us.

We are the members of her Son. She loves the just who are in union with Jesus. She loves sinners, in order to unite them to Jesus. She is always conceiving and forming the Mystical Body. She continues to bestow on Christ's members the affection she lavished on Him: who ever saw such love, such motherhood?

Her happiness in Heaven, far from chilling her love, makes it more ardent. How intensely she desires to save those for whom Jesus died, to see God's family increase and grow in holiness! Her desire fires her prayer. "Prayer for one's neighbor," says St. Thomas, "springs from love." In heaven the saints who are more perfect in charity pray more for those who are on earth, and help them by these prayers. The more they are united to God, the more efficacious their prayers are. The divine order is that the excellence of those who stand higher flows down on those who are lower. That is why St. Paul says of Christ that He is "at the right hand of God, who also maketh intercession for us" (Rom. viii, 34). Our Lady is near Him, united to Him as when He was in the crib and on the cross, exercising her motherhood with love.

(c) It is immeasurably powerful.

One can imagine the power of her intercession. Christian tradition has long called Our Lady: *omnipotentia supplex,* suppliant omnipotence. Mary can do by her prayer all that God can do by His will. Her title of Mother and Mediatrix gives her measureless power with God. "Thy intercession is never repulsed by the Lord," says St. John Damascene; "He refuses none of thy requests, so near art thou to the most simple and adorable Trinity." [8]

St. Thomas tells us how Our Lord prays before His Father: "He intercedes for us, presenting to His Father the humanity that He took for us, and setting forth the desire of His most holy soul for our salvation." [9] So with

---

[8] St. John Damascene, *Homilia in Annuntiatione B. V. Mariae.* J.-P. Migne, *Patrologia Graeca.* XCVI, 647.

[9] *Expositio in Epistolam S. Pauli ad Romanos,* ch. viii, lect. 4.

Our Lady: Mother of God, associated with the Redeemer, she reminds God of her sufferings and her love, sufferings and love so intimately mingled with those of her Son.

The virtual omnipotence of this prayer is measured by the merit and the holiness of Our Lady. It surpasses by far the prayer of the other saints. "What all can do with thee, thou canst do alone, without them," says St. Anselm. "If thou remain silent, no one will pray for us, no one will help me. But pray thou and others will pray and will help me." [10]

It was given to St. Gertrude in a gracious vision to see how powerful Mary's prayer is. "During the singing of the versicle *Ora pro populo,* the Queen of Virgins went up (to the throne of God), knelt reverently, and spoke as mediatrix between God and the congregation, praying most devoutly for each one. But the King of Kings, her Son, raised her with great deference, and placing her at His side on the throne of grace, gave her unlimited power to command as she pleased." [11]

From her prayer we receive everything. Everything that we need for the life divine: grace to enter on it; graces to continue and progress in it; the infused virtues, the gifts of the Holy Ghost, special helps to resist temptation, all the divine blessings ordained for our salvation, everything in short comes to us through Mary. We cannot take a

---

[10] St. Anselm, *Orationes ad B.M.V.;* J.-P. Migne, *Patrologia Latina,* CLVIII, 942-967.

[11] *The Herald of Divine Love,* Book IV, Ch. ix.

forward step in the spiritual life except under her influence. All our supernatural progress depends on her since it is by the grace that she dispenses that we advance. It is she who presides over the formation and increase of the mystical Christ, over the formation of the Church and the saints. For the Church, the Mystical Body of Jesus is the mustard seed ever growing, and Mary watches over that growth, as she watched over the growth of the physical body of Jesus at Bethlehem and Nazareth.

Whether we think of it or not, we are unbrokenly under Mary's influence. The mediation of the Saviour is, by right, the only absolutely necessary mediation. But since it has pleased Providence to associate Mary's mediation so intimately with that of her Son, and not to grant any grace but through her, her mediation has in fact become necessary for us. "She distributes all good things to all," says St. Albert the Great. "This is the economy of the graces that flow down on the human race," says St. Bernardine of Siena. "God is their universal source, Christ the universal mediator, Mary the universal distributor. The Blessed Virgin is the mystical neck of our divine Head; it is through that organ that the heavenly gifts are communicated to the rest of the body." [12]

"The Holy Spirit communicated His ineffable gifts to Mary His faithful Spouse, and He chose her to be the dispenser of all His possessions. Consequently she distributes

---

[12] St. Bernardine of Siena, *Sermo x in Quadragesima.*

all those gifts and graces to whomsoever she wills, in the measure she wills, as she wills and as long as she wills; and there is no heavenly gift that does not pass through her virginal hands. For such is the will of God, who willed that we should receive everything through Mary." [13]

This perpetual dependence on Our Lady and on her mother-love is a motive for great trust and joy. "When I least thought of it," relates Blessed Angela of Foligno, "I was rapt in spirit and I saw the Blessed Virgin in glory. That a woman could be placed on such a throne and in such majesty, flooded me with ineffable joy . . . She stood, praying for the human race. The fittingness that springs from goodness, the fittingness that springs from power gave an inexpressible virtue to her prayer. I was transported with happiness at the sight of that prayer." [14]

"I am the coadjutor of eternal love," said Our Lady to St. Veronica. "I am the guardian and mistress of thy soul: through me thou wilt learn to love." [15]

2. Our Lady acts upon us.

What do we mean when we teach that all graces come to us through Mary? Not that grace perchance, like some precious gift, passes through her hands from God to us:

---

[13] St. Louis Mary Grignion de Montfort, *Op. cit.,* Part I, ch. 1.

[14] Blessed Angela of Foligno, *The Book of Visions,* ch. XLIV. Hello's translation.

[15] Désiré des Planches, *Le Journal de Sainte Véronique Giuliani,* p. 259.

we must not imagine grace in a material fashion, like water, for example, flowing from the divine ocean into our souls through Mary as the aqueduct. Grace is a quality: it is produced in the soul. And Mary receives from God the power of producing grace in us by the operation of the Holy Ghost.

In reality this is another aspect of Mary's intercession. This intercession is a limitless power over us given her by God. It is the active exercise of her maternal protection. "O Queen," said Dante, "who canst what thou willest." God has decreed that Mary's prayer should be a command. In presence of the Trinity that prayer is a supplication which shows her dependence on God and the union of her will with the divine will. In our regard it is the sign of her power of motherhood and the sign efficacious for grace. By interceding, Our Lady produces grace in us. Her prayer is an act that produces life. When she prays, she forms saints.

Plainly, this influence of Our Lady has its special character. It is a prayer, but an efficacious, a sovereign prayer; a prayer that becomes a power actively exercised for the extension of the kingdom of God; a priestly prayer in short, in close connection always with the will of God. Mary is Christ's helper: like Him and with Him she acts incessantly on the saints.

In her and by her efficacious action, the humanity of Jesus was formed; in her also and with her active coöperation the Holy Spirit forms the members of His humanity. "God the Holy Ghost, being sterile in the Godhead, that is, not generating any other divine person, became fertile through her whom He espoused. With her and in her and of her He produced His masterpiece which is God made man; with her and in her and of her He produces every day, until the end of the world, the predestined and the members of the Body of that adorable Head. That is why the more He finds Mary, his beloved and inseparable spouse, in a soul, the more operative He becomes and the more powerful to produce Jesus Christ in that soul, and that soul in Jesus Christ." [16]

What constitutes this action of Our Lady? Think of what she did for Jesus during his earthly life. She conceived Him, watched over His growth, offered Him to God, presented Him to men; she stood by Him in His immolation. That is what she still does for the Mystical Body. All her mysteries are renewed in our favor. The Incarnation, the Presentation, the compassion, continue every day for the formation of the members of Christ.

To know how deep and intimate her action is, we must remember that she is a mother: she conceives us and engenders us in the life of grace. Thence we may determine the character of Mary's action: it is maternal. It is hidden, it works in the privacy of the soul. It reminds one of the influence of the Eucharist in the Church. The Host, which

---

[16] St. Louis Mary Grignion de Monfort, *Op. cit.*, Art II, ii, 20.

is apparently nothing, is yet the life of Christendom. Like her Son, Our Lady is veiled in silence, but she acts incessantly by an interior influence. It is a law of the spiritual life that the higher and deeper an influence is, the more profoundly intimate it is. The silent influence of Mary is the leaven which makes us rise above our sinfulness, the ferment which starts up our activity.

IV. The Presence of Our Lady in Our Life.

We have seen that Our Lady is ever present in the Church. She acts on the life of the Mystical Body. The liturgy applies to her the words of Proverbs (viii, 30): "I was with Him forming all things: playing before Him at all times . . . and my delights were to be with the children of men." What part has she in the workings of the providence of God? She governs men, she rules Christendom and watches over its diverse phases, sometimes so critical: she provides for its needs and responds to its appeals; she leads all things to the successful issue which is the formation of the Mystical Body. And that, the Holy Spirit tells us, is "a play" for her: that universal action on creation, of which the thought makes one dizzy, does not exceed the unique power of the Mother of God. Her immense sway is exercised every moment by perfect acts, diverse and multiple, strong and tender, reaching out to each soul and to the whole Christ whom she envelops in love. Her hidden action, so gentle and delicate, is ever imperceptibly operative on the created universe. One of the realities that the Church was quickest to feel was the guidance of Our Lady's invisible action and her all-pervading maternal influence.

She is present to every soul, with a spiritual presence that is a beautiful reality. Mary is with us because she sees us, loves us, looks after us. She is near us, nearer than our Guardian Angel, nearer in a sense than we are to ourselves; she has a perfect knowledge of each of her children, whose vocation and most hidden secrets are known to her. She penetrates that part of us that we hide from everyone and sometimes do not even know. She has every means of intervening in our daily life and of directing it. And it is so easy to approach her! Between her and us there can be a true exchange of thought and love.

Some persons perhaps will think of the distance that separates us from her glorified body. But what does space matter? God's universal presence bridges all distances, His might abolishes separation. We know that two beings may be side by side in body and yet strangers to each other. Presence begins with knowledge; intimacy springs from the intelligence and the heart. Are we not ever united to Mary by thought and love? We speak to her, she hears us: we invoke her help, she answers by grace; she is in permanent contact with her children. She sees everything, provides for everything. She is present to us as the mother is present to the child that she has conceived and bears in her womb.

Some of her servants have also spoken of a special presence

of Our Lady in the soul. St. Louis Mary Grignion de Mont-fort speaks of it in *Mary's Secret:* "Beware of giving way to anxiety if you do not immediately enjoy the sweet presence of Mary within you. This grace is not given to all, and when God in His great mercy favours a soul with it, it is easily lost unless the soul is faithful to frequent recollection." Elsewhere, speaking more clearly, the saint calls this presence: "dwelling in Mary's fair soul." St. Philip Neri, St. Ignatius, M. Olier, and others, habitually enjoyed this presence.

Let your soul acquire the habit of living with Mary, of acting in union with her intentions, with her love, of going to God through His Mother; be yourself present to Mary by faith. And surely this presence of Mary, which is a precious grace, yet not, it seems, an extraordinary occurrence in Christian life—which, to put it shortly, is a presence of influence and love—will become a blessed reality in your life and the starting-point of fresh progress upwards on the spiritual road.

This spiritual presence of Mary in souls and in the Mystical Body is one of the greatest and loveliest realities of the life of the Church.

CHAPTER THREE

Our Lady Makes Us Grow Through The Sacraments.

I. The Christian Life is a Sacramental Life.

II. Our Lady is at the Well-Spring of the Sacraments.

III. Our Lady Prepares Us for the Sacraments.

      1. Humility and the spirit of poverty.

      2. Charity.

      3. The desire of God.

IV. We Must Approach the Altar with Our Lady.

I. The Christian Life is a Sacramental Life.

The sacraments also give increase to our life. The sacraments are a wonderful means of sanctification. They are indeed the normal means by which God leads men to holiness. They are the principal springs of life, those that Isaias foretold (xii, 3): "You shall draw waters with joy out of the Saviour's fountains": the springs of Calvary, the wounds of Christ. All life comes from His Blood.

It is Christ's humanity that sanctifies us through the sacraments. "The unsearchable riches of Christ," as St. Paul says (Eph. iii, 8), come to us through them. "Virtue went out from Him and healed all" (Luke vi, 19), says the

Gospel. It is the same today when we draw near to Him with confidence: like the woman in the Gospel, we experience the same saving effect: "Somebody hath touched Me, for I know that virtue is gone out from Me" (Luke viii, 46).

The Christian life is a sacramental life. We are born in a sacrament, we are nourished by a sacrament, we are healed by a sacrament, our life is fortified by a sacrament. Some sacraments mark us with the seal of Christ. If we are united to Christ it is through their effect on us: the purpose of each is to unite us to Him and to make the bond of union ever closer.

It causes a kind of stupefaction to note this development of life through the sacraments: the growth of Christ in souls. "He who commanded the light to shine out of darkness hath shined in our hearts" (II Cor. iv, 6).

The soul grows, models itself on Jesus, and at last reaches "unto the measure of the age of the fulness of Christ" (Eph. iv, 13).

II. Our Lady is at the Well-Spring of the Sacraments.

Now, this growth through the sacraments too is given us through Mary's intervention. Certainly, the sacraments produce their effects of themselves in anyone who receives them fittingly. We must not think of any intervention between the sacramental sign and the effect produced. Not in that sense do we think of Mary's intervention.

But whence do the sacraments come, and the life that

they produce in the soul? From the inexhaustible spring that Jesus, with Mary, set flowing on Calvary. The sacraments are a sign of the Passion of Christ, they bring us the grace of Calvary; and Mary suffered in order to co-merit that grace.

Whence come the right dispositions for receiving the sacraments? From Mary's intercession. The complete economy of grace comprises sacramented grace; Mary coöperated in making that economy a reality, she now coöperates in its dispensation.

She is a mother, mother of the members of Christ, mother of the Church. A mother's mission is to diffuse life. But her motherhood is not revealed by outward signs; we never see Mary visibly active in the distribution of the sacraments nor in the means used by the ministers. She has not the priestly power; but the priesthood, instituted and quickened by Jesus, leans on her maternity in its ministry.

Mary is called to union with the divinity in order to give birth to the children of God. Her motherhood corresponds to the fatherhood of God: God has taken a helper of un-imaginable dignity who carries out His will of raising up sons of adoption, brothers of Jesus. He has created a motherhood which takes nothing away from the operation of His fatherhood.

In the last resort, why are there sacraments? In order to give life to the members of the Mystical Body and to preserve and develop it. But does not Our Lady coöperate in that work? The office of motherhood is to form life and to join together the members that will form the body. Mary is the fashioner of the unity of the members of Christ. In her womb, the divinity and humanity were united in the person of Jesus; under her influence too the Mystical Christ attains unity. It is Mary who acts in the formation of life; hers are the hidden operations of motherhood.

St. Leo, speaking of baptism and the other sacraments, asserts that the intervention of the Holy Ghost which makes them efficacious is the extension of His operation in the womb of Our Lady. "The same virtue of the Most High, the same operation of the Holy Ghost which caused Mary to give birth to the Saviour, causes the regenerating water to give birth to the Christians." [1]

So true is it that everything began in Mary's womb, with her collaboration.

What are the sacraments, after all, but purely and simply the humanity of Christ engaged in sanctifying us? That humanity is God's great sacrament, the "river of water of life" of which the Apocalypse speaks (xxii, 1). Now it was given to us through Mary. "From her, the first origin of the blood of Jesus," says Bossuet, "began to pour out the glorious flood of grace which flows into our veins

---

[1] St. Leo, *In Nativitate Domini Sermo* VI. J.-P. Migne, *Patrologia Latina,* LIV, 211.

through the sacraments and carries the spirit of life into the whole body of the Church." Mary is at the fountain head of the sacraments. They apply to us the virtue of the Blood that Jesus received from her.

That is more especially true of the Eucharist. The Body veiled in the sacrament is the Body born of the Virgin Mary, as the liturgy constantly repeats to us. The Eucharist is the great gift of Our Lady. "Here, beloved brethren," said St. Peter Damian, "consider I beg of you what an obligation we are under to the Blessed Mother of God, and what thanks we owe to her after God for such a benefit. The body of Christ which she conceived and carried in her womb, wrapped in swaddling-clothes, fed with her milk with such maternal love, is the same body that we receive at the altar; it is His blood that we drink in the sacrament of our redemption . . . No human words are capable of worthily praising her from whom the Mediator of God and men took flesh. Whatever honor we may give her falls short of her merit, for it is she that prepared in her chaste womb the immaculate flesh that is our food." [2]

Mary desires to give us that food. A mother feeds her children. In the accomplishment of this mystery her will is closely united to the will of the Father and that of the Son, as it was in the mystery of the Incarnation and of the Redemption. The Eucharist, says St. Thomas, is the fulfil-

---

[2] St. Peter Damian, *In Nativitate Beatissimae Virginis Mariae.* J.-P. Migne, *Patrologia Latina,* CXLIII, 743.

ment of the divine giving: *divinae donationis complementum*. At the beginning of that giving, when God so loved the world that He gave His only Son, and when the Son gave Himself and delivered Himself up, Mary also, through love, at Bethlehem, in the Temple, on Calvary, gave us the Son who was hers. Now that the great gift is given in its fulness and the Son has delivered Himself to be our food, is it not just that she too should be present, with an efficacious part to play, and that she too should give us that "fulfilment of the divine giving," the Eucharistic food?

Many saints have written that it was at Mary's prayer that Jesus instituted the Eucharist. They conceive that on the day of the Incarnation, by assenting to the proposals of God, Mary accepted all the consequences of the Incarnation. In any case, she learned of the Eucharist during the public life, when Jesus solemnly promised it. By associating herself so intimately with the mystery of the Cross, she likewise associated herself with its perpetual prolongation, with the sacrifice of the altar which would make her children share in the fruit of the Blood. Mary then willed us to partake of the bread of life.

The story of P. Hermann's conversion is wellknown. Our Lady appeared to him and said amongst other things: "Come and eat the bread that I formed with the virginal milk of my virginal blood; come and drink the wine that I extracted from my pure blood. If thou wouldst know the mother that thou shouldst choose to follow, look to the fruit, to the food that she gives thee: look at the fruit of my womb." And, showing him the monstrance: "See my fruit, the Eucharist."

III. Our Lady Prepares Us for the Sacraments.

But we must approach the sacraments with the necessary dispositions. Grace will produce its fruit if it meets with no obstacles; its fruit will be more abundant according as our dispositions are more perfect. Each one of us receives Christ whole and entire in Communion: some seem to derive little permanent fruit from it, while others, who are better disposed, are as it were flooded with divine life.

Here it is that Our Lady's intervention is sovereignly efficacious. The dispositions for the reception of the sacraments are obtained for us by Mary's prayer, and are distributed by her, as are indeed all graces.

She adorns us with the dispositions and the virtues that God wants to find in us: mothers are accustomed to try to make their children attractive. We find in the *Revelations* of St. Gertrude a lovely story of what Our Lady does to prepare her children for the sacraments:

"During the Mass at which Gertrude was to communicate she saw the Mother of Our Lord shining with the splendor and majesty of all the virtues; and humbly prostrate at her feet, she begged Our Lady to deign to dispose her for receiving the sacrament of the Body of her Son. Then the Blessed Virgin gave her a beautiful necklace which had as it were seven rays. From each of these hung a stone of great price. And these stones indicated the singular virtues that had pleased Our Lord in the Blessed Virgin . . . . When St. Gertrude appeared before God wearing that necklace. Our Lord took such delight in the brilliancy of those virtues that He seemed to be transported with love; He leaned towards Gertrude and drew her to Him with a divine embrace, and, having as it were gathered her in His arms, honored her with His pure and chaste caresses." [3]

1. Humility and the Spirit of Poverty.

St. Gertrude, enumerating the virtues obtained for her by Our Lady, speaks first of humility.

We must always go back to the Incarnation. It is the starting-point of the mystery of Christ, and holds a capital place in our spiritual life. "The Incarnation," says Bèrulle, "is a mystery that binds God to man and man to God; and we must bind ourselves to that mystery . . . it is efficacious and operative and we must bring forth its fruit and receive its effects." Now, "the characteristic grace of the Incarnation is a grace of proverty of spirit and of crosses, a grace of self-renunciation and self-abasement." [4]

Mary was filled with that grace. Her penetrating faith

---

[3] *Vie et révélations de Ste. Gertrude,* Vol II, p. 96. (Gabalda).
[4] Cardinal Pierre de Bérulle, *Oeuvres,* pp. 914, 922.

lit up for her the greatness of God and, in a reflected way, her own nothingness. "Dost thou know who thou art and who I am"? said the Lord to Catherine of Siena. "I am He who is, and thou are she that is not." No one ever better understood or loved that truth than Our Lady. God was all: she was nothing. Mary not only saw that, but she loved to have it so. She saw clearly that she was only what God willed her to be. She loved that absolute dependence on Him. In that light, no motion of self-satisfaction was possible; she was far from attributing any spiritual gift whatever to herself. As her amazing purity sheltered her from every inordinate movement of sense, so her humility sheltered her from every inordinate movement of spirit. She was a woman poor in spirit, detached from self, having relinquished possession of self. Utterly submissive to God, turned wholly towards God, She waited for God. And the Most High overshadowed her and she conceived the Word. *Virginitate placuit, humilitate concepit,* says St. Bernard: "God was pleased by her virginity, by her humility she conceived Him."

Speaking of the Mass, Père de Condren says: "We must sink ourselves in that action and be simply members of Jesus Christ." That is the spirit of renunciation, of detachment from self, the spirit of the Incarnation. The sacraments, communion, will enable us to "put on Christ," as St. Paul says (Gal. iii, 27), on condition that we strip off self.

Are you waiting for God, do you want to be made like to God? Strip yourself of self. Follow Our Lady in her self-renunciation, in her humility. Humility will put you in your place before God. It is the basis of all our relations with God: *locus gratiae* as the saints say, the place in which God distributes His grace. What permanent effect could the sacraments have in a soul full of self, unconvinced of its own wretchedness? Hardly any. "For humility," says St. Thomas, "is the disposition which gives the soul easy access to spiritual and divine goods." [5] Who are they that receive permanent fruit from the sacraments? The poor in spirit, the humble, and only they. Humility is a primary condition for the receiving of the divine gifts.

Let Our Lady train us in that detachment from ourselves, that true humility which fills the heart, which makes us love our dependence and gives us the urgent desire to serve God, to love and glorify Him.

2. CHARITY.

The Eucharist, the term of all the sacraments, is the sacrament of unity and charity. St. Paul wrote to the Corinthians (1 Cor. x, 17): "We, being many, are one bread, one body, all that partake of one bread." "Understand and rejoice," adds St. Augustine. "Unity, piety, charity. 'One bread'. And what is this one bread? A single body made

---

[5] *Summa Theologica,* IIa IIae, q. 161, a. 5, ad 4.

up of many parts. Remember that bread is not made of a single grain of wheat, but many. During the exorcisms you were in some sort under the grindstone. In baptism you were as it were impregnated with water. The Holy Ghost entered into you like the fire that bakes the dough. Be what you see, and receive what you are . . . As to the chalice, many grapes hang in the bunch, but the juice which flows from them is mingled in unity." [6]

We see that charity is essential to the Mystical Body of Christ. We must remember it when we approach the altar. Our participation in the sacrifice must be that of brothers. It would be a mistake to think that communion is our own affair, merely an act of personal devotion. We must not isolate ourselves with Jesus alone. We must think of His members. Communion must be first of all an act of the Mystical Body. To be in communion with the head of the Mystical Body is to be in communion with the members, for they are one. "He who desires to live," says St. Augustine, "knows where he will enjoy life, where he will find the well of life. Let him draw near and believe, let him become one with Christ, and he will find life. But let him not shrink from uniting with His other members." [7]

We see that unity and fraternal charity are absolutely necessary. We should never try to approach the sacraments if we have not brotherly love in our hearts. "If thou offer

[6] *Sermon* 172.
[7] *In Joann.* xxvi, 13.

thy gift at the altar, and there thou remember that thy brother hath anything against thee, leave there thy offering before the altar and go first to be reconciled to thy brother: and then coming thou shalt offer thy gift" (Matt., v, 23-24). But if you have "bowels of mercy," as the Apostle says (Col. iii,12), if your heart is full of forgiveness and love, come and open your soul: God will fill it with His life, and you will hear Jesus repeat the amazing words: "Holy Father, keep them in Thy name . . . that they all may be one, as Thou, Father, in Me, and I in Thee; that they also may be one in Us, that the world may believe that Thou has sent Me" (John xvii, 11, 21).

3. THE DESIRE OF GOD.

It is of God's essence to give Himself. Does not the beatitude of the Father and the Son consist in that substantial love which proceeds from their mutual delight, the gift that they give each to the other? But it is an astounding mystery, that God should also give Himself to creatures. The Father gives us His Son. Both together give us the Holy Ghost, who is, as the liturgy says, the gift of the Most High to the world.

Thus life is a communion. It is a communion in God: the Father gives Himself eternally to the Word who in this communion receives the divine nature whole and entire. The Father and the Word together breathe the breath of infinite love, who is the Holy Spirit.

It is a communion in the mystery of the Incarnation. From the first moment of His existence in Mary's womb the humanity of Christ was taken possession of by the person of the Word. The divinity assumed the humanity and so an eternal communion began between divinity and humanity.

Such also we might say was Our Lady's communion. When God overshadowed her, she received Jesus in His divinity and His humanity. And with a spontaneous impulse she gave all that she was to welcome God. She answered with an all-embracing assent: *ecce ancilla.* She teaches us to receive God.

God then wills to impart Himself. But, in the divine plan of the Incarnation, we can only find God, we can only share His life, through Our Lady. Through her the shepherds and the Magi could be admitted to the crib of the God-Child and contemplate Him with the eyes of the body. That is far truer when we want to contemplate Him with the eyes of the heart and to unite with Him. God gives Himself through Mary. The gift of God to men, Christ Jesus, the source of our life, is the gift of Mary also. The Apostles' Creed tells us that Jesus was conceived of the Holy Ghost and born of the Virgin Mary. What was true at the beginning will remain true to the end of time: wherever Jesus is born by grace, He is born of the Holy Ghost and of the Virgin Mary. The Incarnation gave Our Lady power to communicate Christ. Every time that she draws near to a soul, it is to give it her Son.

Corresponding to the will of Jesus to share His life with those who have become His members, there should be in us the desire to receive Him. We know that this grace to feel the desire of God comes from her who, immediately after conceiving Jesus, rose in haste to go and carry Him to John the Baptist. She kindles the hunger for God in our hearts, and especially the longing for the Eucharist which gives her Son to us. Not a sensible longing, such as some saints have experienced, but a spiritual desire, a will intent on the spiritual food which will draw our union with God closer, renew our strength, calm our passions.

Nothing does us more good than that desire of God. It is by far the best preparation for the sacraments. God gives Himself to all who call upon Him: "If any man thirst," said Jesus (John vii, 37), "let him come to Me and drink." To St. Mechtilde He said: "The bees do not fly to suck honey out of the flowers with as much eagerness as bears Me towards thy soul when it desires to receive Me." [8]

When we receive the sacraments, grace is imparted to the soul according to the energy of its desires. The more we expect, the more we get. For desire born of humility removes obstacles: it opens the door of the soul and the lovely words of the Apocalypse are realized: "Behold, I stand at the gate and knock. If any man shall hear My voice and open to Me the door, I will come in to him, and

---

[8] St. Mechtilde, *Révélations,* p. III, chap. iii. Oudin, 1877.

will sup with him, and he with Me" (Apoc. iii, 20).

We should live in a state of desire, aspiring to God. St. Gregory of Nyssa said: "God thirsts for our thirst."

IV. We Must Approach the Altar with Our Lady.

That is the daily advice of the Church in the Canon of the Mass; *communicantes et memoriam venerantes in primis gloriosae semper Virginis Mariae.*

What do we seek when we go to the altar?

We seek Emmanuel, Him who deigned to become "God with us," whose real presence is the strength of our life, "the fountain of living water," as the Scripture says (Jerem. ii, 13). But to whom do we owe this real presence of Emmanuel but to Mary his Mother, whose humility and purity have drawn Him down? Who will give us access to Him but she whose mission it is to present Christ to the world, who gave Him to John the Baptist, to the shepherds, the Magi, Simeon? It is she who gives us Jesus.

We go to the altar still more to have a share in the sacrifice. "We are sanctified by the oblation of the body of Jesus Christ once" (Hebr. x, 10). All graces, all holiness come from the cross, and therefore from the Mass which perpetuates the cross. The altar is Calvary: the same offering is offered, the same Victim is presented by the same High Priest. Who will give us access to that sacrifice which gives us Christ in the totality of His mysteries?

Our Lady. From her come the Priest and the Victim.

It was in Mary's womb that the humanity of Christ received the unction of the Holy Ghost, that sacerdotal anointing that flower over Jesus like an "oil of gladness" (Ps. 44); an anointing that made Him our "priest for ever" (Ps. 109). The Holy Ghost shall come upon thee, said the Angel to Our Lady, and He that shall be born of thee shall be the Holy One. May thy word be fulfilled, said Mary, "Fiat," giving the signal for that anointing and consecration of the eternal Priest.

She gives us the Victim. She willed to give birth to the Saviour, to Him who would save us from our sins. The Victim began to offer Himself in her womb. St. Paul assures us that that was the first word He spoke at the very moment of His incarnation: "A body Thou has fitted to me; holocausts for sin did not please Thee. Then said I: Behold I come" (Heb. x, 5-7).

The *Consummatum est* of the cross is only the completion of the *Ecce venio* spoken in Mary's womb. Our Lady knew that she was the mother of the Victim.

All her life she offered that Victim, and especially on Calvary. Since the Mass is the continuation of Calvary, Mary is present at it, inseparable from the divine Victim. She still gives us the High Priest and the Host. When we receive the Body that is sacrificed on the altar, and the Blood that redeems us, how can we possibly not think of

Mary? That Body was formed in her; she gave that Blood to her Son. Through her the Word became our food.

St. John Damascene called Mary "the priestly virgin." We can see why. Not that she received the priestly character of the sacrament. But her maternity stamped her with a sacred stamp. She had the spirit of her Son our Redeemer which is eminently the spirit of the priesthood. She cannot speak the sacramental words over the bread. But in her own name she spoke that far-reaching *Fiat* which gave Jesus to the world. She it is who, on behalf of God, distributes the divine life. She is the universal mediatrix, the Mother of the Sovereign Priest and of the Victim.

The Mass is the great act of the Church; it is the essential act of the Body of Christ. Our Lady is there in union with the Church to distribute the fruits of the Blood of Christ.

Our Lady Makes Us Grow By Merit.

I. We Grow by Merit.

Our life can increase rapidly by merit. The grace of God is a principle of growth in us. Just as Jesus grew in His personal humanity when He was on earth, He desires to grow in us His members, and to reach the perfect age. We must, "doing the truth in charity . . . in all things grow up in Him the Head, even Christ" (Eph. iv, 15).

We grow by love. Love transforms everything, even

53

the most ordinary actions. If a Christian is united with Christ and does His will, that is enough to give sovereign importance to his life and measureless value to his actions. No matter how ordinary, how easy, how humble, they are, when done through love they are supernatural acts: they give glory to God and draw down His presence.

We do not sufficiently reflect that it is easy for a Christian to increase his grace and to deepen the action of the Holy Trinity in his soul. Grace is always increased by meritorious acts. If through love you perform an act more intently than just through habitual practice of some virtue, your merit is increased, multiplied, and exceeds all your preceding merit. The Trinity deepens the divine life of grace in you. And all that is needed is a very humble act, sometimes a mere movement of the heart, but prompted by charity.

It makes one tremble to think of the perfection that each one of us might attain to. Grace is something so great, so mighty! Fidelity to grace unlocks, so to say, God's generosity: if you are faithful to one grace, it brings another more powerful, more efficacious, in its train. God pours Himself out on you afresh. You are swept forward by love.

II. Our Lady Lived the Christian Life.

Let us look at Our Lady: she lived our life and merited

immense graces by living it, graces that she has in order to impart them to us.

She travelled all the paths that we have to travel. She had all our joys and all our sufferings. She lived all the mysteries of Jesus, coöperated in them: she possesses the fulness of their fruits. That means that all the graces merited for us by Jesus, and which we have to reproduce, are in her and flow ever from her into us, to bring our souls into that life of Christ.

Our Lady was created in the image of Jesus; no creature came so near to reproducing His perfections. All Our Lady's graces, gifts, virtues came from Him. What is more, she reproduced in her life His character and way of acting.

She realized in perfection the likeness to Jesus that we have to acquire. If you want to know how Jesus adored and prayed, how He acted towards His neighbor and towards sinners, His goodness, His condescension, His mercy, His loving intercourse with His friends, the generosity of His love: look at Mary. She is the perfect reflection of Him: she reveals all, reproduces all, with a mother's sweetness.

III.   The Fulness of Grace.

"Thou art full of grace," said the angel of the Incarnation. Our Lady's holiness was immense already. From the first moments of her life God had showered favors on her: she had received the gifts of divine life far beyond all other creatures. She was filled with them to the capacity of her being. That capacity already exceeded anything we can possibly imagine, for God purposed to bring to perfection in His mother all that He proposed to accomplish in His members and to make her the heart of the Church's life.

And yet Mary's grace constantly grew.

Even saints stand still and fall. They mingle their personal tendencies with the operation of God in them. Even in the saints God does not do all that He wills.

But Mary corresponded totally with grace. No fault, no imperfection, ever impeded her spirit's flight. Her will, united to the divine Will, moved onwards with irresistible power. From the moment of her conception she went towards God with deliberate love. She was wholly turned towards God. Every act of her life was dictated by intense love, which grew with every grace. She increased continually in holiness because she increased continually in love. Human imagination is too feeble to follow her progress. Every hour in innumerable ways she rose higher. Nothing of the divine impulsion was lost in her. Grace filled her being more and more as it does in heaven. Every moment the fidelity of her love attracted the Blessed Trinity, which poured its influence out on her afresh. She received a ceaseless influx of divine life.

She acquired this new merit more particularly according as the mysteries of Christ were unfolded.

For example, let us look at what took place in Mary when she carried Jesus in her womb. There was a unique exchange of love. There was first the union of the flesh common to both. Mary gave Jesus her purest flesh to form His body; she gave Him the blood that was to save the world; she formed the heart and the humanity that were to be the abundant source of so many graces. She gave that gift with inexpressible tenderness, with a love lit by the light of Jesus which made her understand the ultimate goal of the mystery. Jesus responded as God alone can. What was happening in Mary's womb resembled what theologians teach about the inner life of the Holy Trinity, that eternal exchange of light and love between the three divine Persons, that circumincession which is the beatitude of God. Similarly, there was between Jesus and His mother a stupendous exchange of affection which God alone can understand. What abundant graces flowed for Mary from that direct and permanent contact with the author of grace! The tie between them was unique, was complete. The mere presence of the Word was a continuous cause of grace, and Mary's perfect dispositions helped to make the outpouring of grace more abundant and never-ending.

Intimate contact with the humanity of Christ demands a spiritual contact by grace still more intimate. "Our Saviour

never shares His bodily presence except with the purpose
of a still closer union in the spirit . . . . If that is so, divine
Virgin, I conceive something so great in thee that not only
I cannot express it, but my mind labors to form an explicit
idea of it.   For thy union with the body of Jesus, when
thou hadst conceived Him in thy womb, was such that no
closer union can be imagined.   If union of spirit did not
correspond to it, the love of Jesus would have been defrauded
of what it had a right to expect, it would have suffered
violence in thee.   To satisfy Him, thou must have been as
closely united to Him in spirit as thou wert by the ties of
nature and of blood.   And since that union was caused by
grace what can one think or say of it?   Is there any limit to
our conceptions if they are not to fall short of such greatness?   And if we add together all the gifts of all creatures,
can they all together equal the plenitude of thy gifts?" [1]
Jesus, says Bérulle, "drew her to Himself, took complete possession of her.   And the two hearts of Jesus and Mary, so
intimately related by nature, were still more intimately
united by grace, and lived in each other." [2]

Thus, throughout her whole life, Our Lady shared in
the mysteries of her Son.   In those mysteries, God little by
little unfolded His hidden designs for the world.   Our
Lady was His confidante.   What was more, she had her
place in them as the collaborator of the Saviour.   She co-

---

[1] Bossuet, *First Sermon on the Nativity of the B.V.M.,* 2nd point.
[2] Cardinal Pierre de Bérulle, *Œuvres,* p. 494.

operated with Him. God gave her special light for that collaboration. And it all increased her merit. Her actions were flooded with light and love. Think, for example, of her merit as she stood at the foot of the Cross. Her Compassion was a work of love: love of God and love of men. She delivered up her Son through love. What boundless merit, and what graces she must have received at the moment that she became, in fact, through her maternity of suffering, the mother of all the children of God!

Add the increase of her merit as her life unrolled itself day by day. Never a stain, never a fall, never a stoppage in the development of her limitless grace, but continual progress. Each act of Our Lady brought about growth in grace. Through love, God flooded her with His lights, and there was no measure but her own ever-growing capacity. "The sower went forth to sow" (Matt. xiii, 3), and sowed His seed every minute; she received it all with docility, with love; she preserved it all and brought forth fruit a hundred-fold. "The years passed," says Bérulle, "graces increased and in that order of grace which was peculiar to her, she entered day by day into an admirable element; she entered it by a special infusion of grace and by perfect coöperation. There was a sacred harmony between the spirit of God and the spirit of Mary. God every moment poured new graces into her soul, and her soul responded incessantly with all its power. And that correspondence and perfect harmony lifted her up to a towering height of grace; and those graces though very great in her soul which was ever advancing in the ways of God, were but steps to raise her to fresh graces. So rare a soul, eminent, divine, living thus on earth, delighted the heavens; and would delight the earth if its darkness did not blind it to so rare a spectacle." [3]

It was love that made the beauty of her life. Our Lady put into her actions so much light and love that they surpassed the most arduous achievements of the greatest saints. "The song of nightingales though they are only young learners, is incomparably more musical than that of the most accomplished goldfinches." [4]

Every minute Mary's burning love received grace, responded to it utterly, used it perfectly, and caused it to be endlessly multiplied.

"Days went on adding themselves to days, and years to years; and like some fabulous machinery, with overwhelming force and with invisible speed, the process of correspondence and sanctification went on, multiplying itself in one short hour beyond the figures of all human sums." [5]

"But as divine love reigned unimpeded in her heart it grew constantly day by day through its own exercise and increased of itself; so that at last, continually extending its domain, it reached such perfection that earth could no

---

[3] Cardinal Pierre de Bérulle, *Vie de Jésus,* ch. V.
[4] St. Francis de Sales, *Traité de l'amour de Dieu.* V. XI, ch. 5.
[5] Frederick Faber, *The Foot of the Cross,* ch. VIII, p. 363, Ed. 1857.

longer contain it. So that there was no other cause for Mary's death than her living, burning love . . . .

"As love was the mainspring of Mary's life, so love was the cause of her death." [6]

IV. Our Lady Distributes that Life.

But Mary is a mother. The glory of a mother is to bring forth children. If God made her so great and capable of containing all the treasures of life, it was that she might give them out. She is the reservoir of divine grace, so that she may become its channel. The blessings she has received must come down on men in the spiritual order of creation. God is in her as a source of life for Christ's members. She has been so richly gifted only that she may give.

Besides, love urges her. The law of love, especially of a mother's love, is to give. Mary overflows with life and blessedness, and we are in need. Can you imagine a true mother who if she were happy would not burn with longing to make her children happy? In truth, Mary distributes to us that life that has passed through her. For us Our Lady is all love, love giving itself.

V. Our Lady Helps Us to Work out Our Christian Vocation.

We can only reach happiness by fulfilling our supernatural vocation. "Blessed be the God and Father of Our Lord

---

[6] Bossuet, *Sermon sur l'Assomption,* V. IV, pp. 412, 424.

Jesus Christ," says St. Paul, "who . . . . chose us in Him before the foundations of the world, that we should be holy and unspotted in His sight in charity" (Eph. i, 3, 4). God thought of us from all eternity, and in His love fixed a perfection to be attained by us: He wants us to become like His Son. "Whom He foreknew, He also predestinated to be made conformable to the image of His Son" (Rom. viii, 29). That is the Christian vocation: to grow conformable to Christ, to become the "image of Christ," to live like Christ.

In what measure has each of us to reproduce in himself the likeness of Jesus? That is God's secret. But Our Lady knows the most mysterious secret of our eternal predestination. She knows the personal vocation of each one of us; she knows what I have to be. Her mother's love is stirred by my spiritual future. She is really my guide, my help, my strength, in the fulfilment of my vocation. The spiritual life is a daily living, it has its moments of growth, but also its surprises, trials, uncertainties, and lapses. The mother of divine grace is the guide of that growth, she guides it with her gentleness, her loving help, her constant discerning care, all her motherly compassion.

First of all, she tries to impel us towards God, to put into us the desire of the divine life. Desire is the beginning of all growth. She remembers her Son Jesus in the porches of the Temple, standing and crying to the multitude: "If any man thirst, let him come to me and drink" (John vii,

37). A Christian seeking God would not take long to find Him. Did not Jesus say to Blessed Angela of Foligno: "If anyone desired to feel Me in his spirit, I would not deny Myself to him. If anyone desired to see Me, with very great pleasure I would show Myself to him. If anyone desired to converse with Me, with very great joy I would converse with him."

Experience is there to tell us that those who live with Our Lady are inspired with greater confidence in the fulfilment of their Christian vocation. St. Paul wished that "rooted and founded in charity, we may be able to comprehend, with all the saints, what is the breadth, and length, and height, and depth; to know also the charity of Christ, which surpasseth all knowledge, that we may be filled unto all the fulness of God" (Eph. iii, 17-19). That presupposes that we should desire that "fulness of God," that we should aspire to that deep union with Jesus.

But the Mother of Grace possesses that fulness for us, and she can make our souls capable of receiving it. It is her mission as mother to make us members of Christ. For that, she will "show you Jesus" every day of your life, and she will teach you to seek Him in the duties of your state, in your work and your sufferings, and in the other members of the mystical Christ.

VI. Our Lady Teaches Us to Work.

"The Son of man," said Jesus, "is not come to be ministered unto, but to minister" (Matt. xx, 28). His mother thought the same. Her life was spent in work.

What did she do? What the women of Nazareth still do. You should see them in their primitive houses, in those rooms up the hillside, hollowed out of the rock, pretty much as Joseph's house was, looking after a very humble household, preparing the meals, grinding the corn, kneading the flour, baking the bread, going to the only fountain of Nazareth to draw the water which, in Galilean fashion, they bring home pitcher on head. Those were the things that she who was blessed amongst women did every day. Her maternal hands that carried the Child Jesus busied themselves diligently with the daily monotonous household tasks. She put her heart into them because God's will was there.

Her work was an act of adoration, of lowly service for the glory of the Lord Most Holy. She performed it with humility and love. For her, to work in weariness was to fulfill all justice. It was an excellent way of bowing not only beneath the will of God, who decreed that man should eat his bread in the sweat of his brow, but of doing homage to the Being of God who had dowered her with such magnificent gifts.

And then was she not the mother of the Redeemer? Like her Son, she devoted herself to the penance of work, toilsome work, the tasks of the poor.

That is the kind of work to which Our Lady invites us: work which becomes an act of religion, a humble recognition of the sovereign rights of God, and also does service to our neighbor. It is right and just that we sinners should expend ourselves, in union with Christ, in the service of Him who has so loved us. It is right and just that Christ's members should labor for one another. Christian work is an exchange of services.

Work is a grievous mystery for the human race: because of original sin, it involves toil, bitter toil. But it is also a mystery of joy. "My Father worketh until now," said Jesus, "and I work" (John v, 17). In our labors let us remember that divine activity. It is partly through work that we collaborate in God's sanctifying operation on the world. When God put man on the earth, creation was complete; but we still have to organize it, to turn it God-wards, to make it sing God's glory. Yes, creation is not so much a spectacle to behold, as a divine work to finish. "For the expectation of the creature," St. Paul tells us, "waiteth for the revelation of the sons of God . . . every creature groaneth and travaileth in pain, even till now" (Rom. viii, 19, 22).

But how are we to work? Think of Nazareth. When Jesus and Mary worked, it was not at the expense of their inner life. Their activity never took from their contemplation. Jesus could always say: "I am in the Father" (John x, 38), whether at St. Joseph's bench or on the roads of Galilee. Our Lady was unbrokenly engaged in contemplating and loving God: that was the permanent background of her innermost life, against which all her exterior actions stood out and all her mysteries flowered. That is what St. Paul asks us to do: "Whatsoever you do in word or in work, do all in the name of the Lord Jesus Christ, giving thanks to the Father by Him" (Col. iii, 17). The work of souls united to God is far more useful for His glory and for men's salvation than that of ordinary Christians, through the charity which inspires them. Their activity ceases to endanger their inner life; their work turns into love. Even absorbing occupations, if they are willed by God, do not lessen such union with the Lord. "When His spirit rules yours," said Ven. Marie de l'Incarnation, "when He has taken possession of your innermost being and holds you in intimate, unbroken union with His divine Majesty because you see Him with the eye of love, all your occupations will be unable to distract you from that divine communion." She added: "I have said your innermost being, because in this world it is not possible to carry on temporal affairs without giving them the fitting attention of judgment and of reason. In that state of union and communion with God in the higher part of the soul, one does not lose His holy presence." [7]

It often happens in these exhausting labors, that charity is not felt, and only guides the supreme point of the will. The servant of God remains none the less in the exercise of love; and "he that abideth in charity, abideth in God, and God in him" (I John iv, 16).

---

[7] *Letter* 99.

VII. Our Lady Teaches Us to Love and Serve Our Neighbor.

Charity to our neighbor is a supernatural and theological virtue, that is to say, one of those higher virtues directly concerned with God. "The love with which we love our neighbor," says St. Thomas, "is of the same kind as that with which we love God." Therefore we are not free to love or not to love our neighbor. Our Lord made it an absolute obligation. "A new commandment I give unto you: that you love one another as I have loved you." Fraternal charity is the precise sign of the Christian. "By this shall all men know that you are my disciples, if you have love one for another" (John xiii, 34-35).

The Eternal Father said to St. Catherine of Siena: "If a soul loves me, it loves its neighbor; otherwise its love is not real, for love of Me and love of the neighbor are one. The more a soul loves Me, the more it loves its neighbor." This union between the love of God and of the neighbor is so close that St. Paul even says: "He that loveth his neighbor hath fulfilled the law" (Rom. xiii, 8). And St. John: "We know that we have passed from death to life, because we love the brethren. He that loveth not abideth in death" (I John iii, 14).

To serve our neighbor is an immediate fruit of union with God. It is the characteristic of goodness to diffuse itself. The infinite Good from the very fact that He exists, gives Himself in the person of the Son and of the Holy Spirit, and even ends by overflowing into creation. Consequently, when a creature shares in that divine goodness it immediately experiences the desire to give itself out to other creatures. The greater its share in that goodness, the more it desires to give. The more God is in it, the more it feels urged to give God. That is the law of the mutual illumination of the angels: because they have a fuller possession of God, the angels of the upper hierarchies hasten to share their lights with the lower angels. It is the same with the saints: the more they know and love God, the more eager they are to share their light and their love with their brethren. So much so that it is perfectly legitimate to judge of the interior state of a soul by its zeal for the service of the neighbor. "O our Resurrection! Mighty and eternal Trinity, expand my soul! O Redeemer! Our Resurrection! Eternal Trinity, always burning, never dying, who canst never grow less even when Thou dost inflame the whole earth . . . . I beseech Thee to stir up my soul and to set it afire for the salvation of the world." [8]

Our Lady had an ardent, boundless love for her neighbor. Her love of the neighbor was so to say an outflow of her love of God. "I pray for them," said Jesus to His Father, "because they are thine" (John xvii, 9). When she contemplated the inexpressible love of God for souls:—the Father, who created them through sheer goodness and magnificently gifted them, calling them to eternal blessedness; the Son, becoming man for them, seeking them in toil and

---

[8] St. Catherine of Siena.

labor, and suffering to make them happy; the Holy Spirit, the Spirit of love and truth, working ceaselessly to make them pure, holy, glorious—when Our Lady contemplated that "excess of love" (as she did at every moment), she felt herself invaded by a limitless love of all souls, children of the Father, members of the Son, tabernacles of the Holy Ghost, who, moreover, were her own children. In her heart she said like Jesus: "I lay down my life for my sheep" (John x, 13).

She lived to minister to us. All her life she prayed for us. Her prayer, it is true, was first of all adoration of the Divinity, thanksgiving; but immediately it turned to supplication for us. She well knew that she was giving God great joy by that prayer: she was affording His divine life the opportunity of pouring itself out, for God waits for prayer to bestow His favors. She was the partner in His mercy.

Our Lady said to the angel that she was the handmaid of the Lord: she might have added that she was the handmaid of men. She did indeed live for us. Her ministry to men has a large place in the great mysteries of her life. Everyone knows that Mary's answer at the Incarnation was an immense act of charity towards men whom she was adopting for her children. Charity made her hasten to Elizabeth. Her charity at Cana urged her Son to forestall His manifestation and to perform His first miracle. Charity made her suffer on Calvary.

What fired that great zeal? In order to understand the real springs of the love of souls, of apostolic fervor, we must go back to what happened in Mary's womb, at the moment of the Incarnation. St. Paul explains it in the epistle to the Hebrews (x, 5-10). When Christ came into the world He said: "Sacrifice and oblation Thou wouldst not, but a body Thou hast fitted to Me; holocausts for sin did not please Thee . . . . Then said I: Behold I come to do Thy will, O God . . . . In the which will," adds St. Paul, "we are sanctified by the oblation of the body of Jesus Christ once." Later Our Lady heard her Son say these surprising words to the apostles, an echo of the *Ecce venio* spoken in her womb: "Therefore doth the Father love me, because I lay down my life" (John x, 17).

God willed to save men by the death of His Son, and because Jesus accepted that will His Father loved Him. The apostolate, the service of the neighbor, consists first of all then in the sacrifice which communicates divine life. For that sacrifice, which gives glory to God, the Word was made flesh: "Father, for this cause I came unto this hour. Father, glorify Thy name" (John xii, 27).

Think now of the union between Jesus and Mary, and you will understand the intensity of her zeal. She, too, said her *Ecce venio,* which consisted in offering her Son for us. All the limitless grace of being mother of the Mystical Body involves her in sacrifice, and therefore in the apostolate. She wants to shed abroad the divine life, to give glory to God by making members of Christ.

And so we understand that the service of our neighbor does not consist in fussy activity, but above all in prayer and sacrifice. The spirit of sacrifice is the spirit of true apostles: true apostles are those who give themselves out in the charity of Christ. That is why Our Lady is the Queen of Apostles.

VIII. Union with Our Lady in Daily Life by the Spirit of Obedience.

Two words of Jesus sum up His whole life, the words that He spoke as He came into the world: *"Ecce venio*: My God, behold I come to do Thy will." Mary's whole life is likewise summed up in the words that she spoke to the archangel: "Behold the handmaid of the Lord." Both Jesus and Mary lived in accordance with those words spoken at the beginning of their mission, the mighty spontaneous utterance of their humility, expressing the fundamental condition of their souls. They were obedient, obedient, the Scripture tells us, "unto death, even the death of the Cross" (Phil. ii, 8). All their filial love of the Father revealed and fulfilled itself in loving and unlimited obedience. "My meat is to do the will of Him that sent me. I do always the things that please Him" (John iv, 34; viii, 29).

Our Lady calls us to that spirit of obedience. It is the proof, the supreme proof, of love. "He that hath My commandments and keepeth them," says Jesus, "he it is

that loveth Me.   And he that loveth Me shall be loved
of My Father; and I will love him, and will manifest Myself
to him" (John xiv, 21).   Everyone of us is obliged to love.
But who can assert that he loves?   Certain persons of lively
sensibility might believe that they are advanced on the
spiritual ascent because they are quick to tears and promises.
The words of Jesus safeguard us against uncertainty as to
our sentiments: love is in obedience.

This obedience puts us in union with God: "he shall be
loved of My Father."   Dependence on God grounds us in
close fidelity to God.   Love practised, proved, faithful, gives
rise to mutual trust, to intimate possession.   The obedient
Christian, delighting in the will of God, surrendering himself to His rights, is, St. Paul says, "one and the same spirit"
(I Cor. xii, 11).   He draws his sustenance from God: "God
is a perpetual communion to the soul that does His will,"
said St. Vincent de Paul.

Jesus said an astonishing thing about obedience, and
precisely apropos of Our Lady: "Whosoever shall do the
will of My Father . . . . he is My brother and sister and
mother" (Matt. xii, 50).   "He is my mother: He conceives
the Word spiritually by faith," says St. Bede, "he brings
the Word to birth and feeds Him, by doing what is right,
in his own heart and the heart of his neighbor."   There is
the Christian's great task: bringing God to birth.

One can guess the merit of the soul that lives in that

spirit of obedience. Its least actions are holy. There is no such thing now as a commonplace and insignificant life: obedience makes everything worthy of God. It was through obedience that the lowly life of Our Lady gave such glory to God. When a Christian follows the will of God, he is no longer ever alone, he can say with Jesus: "He that sent Me is with Me and He hath not left Me alone . . . The Father who abideth in Me, He doth the works" (John viii, 29; xiv, 10).

The life of Our Lady was a perfect and constant assent to the divine will, a plenary assent which gave her up to God: wherefore the Father was able to accomplish His great mystery through her. Our Lady leads us too to fulfil our vocation through obedience. Did not St. Paul say: "This is the will of God, your sanctification" (I Thess. iv, 3)? The Trinity works ceaselessly to accomplish that will. Think of what would happen if God, through our dispositions, suffered no opposition in bringing His desire to fruition! How abundant His graces would be the day that our obedience responded to His love! And what joy for Our Lady to see God's great designs fulfilled, to see the total Christ completed in the saints!

CHAPTER FIVE

Our Lady Makes Us Grow Through Prayer.

I.   Our Lady Prepares Us for Prayer.

   1. The reverential prayer of Christ and of His Mother.

   2. Interior purity:

     (a) Silence;

     (b) Renunciation.

II. Our Lady Teaches Us to Pray in Joy.

   1. Mary's joys.

   2. Our joys.

   3. Our Lady shows us how to take these joys.

   4. Our Lady unites us with the joy of Jesus and her own:

     (a) The joy of adoration;

     (b) The joy of glorification;

     (c) The joy of gratitude.

III. Our Lady Teaches Us to Pray in Faith.

   1. Jesus goes away.

   2. The prayer of faith.

   3. Following Our Lady.

   4. Prayer in the night.

I. Our Lady Prepares Us for Prayer.

1. THE REVERENTIAL PRAYER OF CHRIST AND OF HIS MOTHER.

"The hour cometh and now is," said Jesus to the Samaritan woman, "when the true adorers shall adore the Father in spirit and in truth. For the Father also seeketh such to adore Him" (John IV, 23). Jesus came on earth to form and gather to Himself those adorers in spirit and in truth who would give the Godhead the perfect worship that the Heavenly Father was waiting for from the creation of the world. The first creature that perfectly responded to His desires was His mother: Our Lady, uniting herself to the adoration, the life, the sacrifice of her Son; surrendering herself with Him in order to establish the reign of God on earth, was the perfect adorer.

What does it mean to adore God in spirit and in truth? It means giving God's infinite rights the full response of human intelligence and will. It means honoring God as He has revealed Himself to us; prostrating ourselves in deep humility before His perfection; reverencing Him, praising Him, rejoicing in His happiness; devoting ourselves in joy to the accomplishment of His will. It means the full homage of submission and love.

Such was the adoration of Jesus. His inner life was incessant adoration. A mighty movement urged Him to abase Himself before His Father is a sort of interior annihilation. As man, Jesus held His perfection from the munificence of God; He was a creature, that is to say nothingness. Overwhelmed at the sight of so many benefits received by His humanity, He had the urge unceasingly to acknowledge the fulness of divine sovereignty. He rejoiced in praising God and confessing the infinite perfections of God; He found His delight and His rest in them. Jesus spent Himself wholly in that incessant adoration, which was not merely loving recognition of God's infinite rights, but joyous self-abandonment to those rights and a burning need to spend Himself for God's glory. No creature ever more humbly abased himself before God's majesty; no creature ever experienced more reverence for the divine perfection, or felt a greater desire to sacrifice himself for the glorification of God.

That is why even in the womb of His mother He said: "Father, behold I come to do Thy will"; that is why He was so humble, even towards men. Justice demanded it, as well as His love. He passed, not as one ministered to, but as one ministering; as a workman. "Pride, melt at this sight! Jesus, the son of a carpenter, Himself a carpenter, known by His trade, with no reference to any other occupation or activity." [1]

Our Lady united herself intimately to the religious submission of her Son. She followed Him in his mysteries,

---

[1] Bossuet.

because she was His mother and united to Him by her state in the work of redemption. Now, in each of these mysteries, their first work in common was to seek the glory of God, to obey, to adore. The same need of adoration and humiliation prostrated them before God.

Our Lady abased herself in thanksgiving: "The Lord hath regarded the lowliness of His handmaid," she said to her cousin. She saw the Lord bending down to her natural weakness to make of her His masterpiece, the mother of His Son; He filled her full of grace and purity. But it was all the gratuitous gift of love. As Jesus in her womb said: *"Ecce venio,* behold I come," she repeated after him: "Behold the handmaid of the Lord," thus expressing the habitual disposition of her soul.

She was, like Jesus, to surrender herself completely to the will of God. She was to offer herself with Him, to suffer, to pray like Him. She too plunged into an abyss of humility, into a sort of annihilation before Him who, though He poured out graces on her, yet remained the Lord.

For that reason she sought obedience, particularly humiliating obedience, in order by her acts of self-abasement to pay constant homage to the majesty of God. She willed to unite with the religious reverence of Her Son; it was a necessity of her mother love. She knew that her Son was a victim offering Himself for the glory of His Father: she followed Him in His humiliation. Jesus would come into the world, not as the glorious Son of God, but as the victim of the sins of men. Mary associated herself with this state of abasement and "accepted to be the humiliated mother of a humiliated Son." [2]

Mary associates us with this reverential spirit of her Son. She inspires the soul that submits to her influence with the humility from which spring true adoration and love. Without that basic humility piety would be nothing but an illusion. God loves us infinitely, and seizes every opportunity of showing us His tenderness. But He is God, the Infinite, He before whom every creature is nothing: the first just attitude is to adore Him. If a Christian has any true knowledge of the Godhead, however slight, he feels the imperious urge to adore, to fall prostrate, and to say with Jesus: "Holy Father!" That humble and loving adoration is the summit of Christian worship. It is triumphant in heaven, where the saints fall prostrate and cast their crowns before the throne of God. That adoration is the spontaneous movement of love before the Infinite. It is the fruit of divine light: "It is the light of humility that gives birth to love. The soul, seeing its nothingness, and God bending down to that nothingness, and God's heart embracing that nothingness, takes fire, is transformed, and adores." [3]

---

[2] Cardinal de Bérulle, *Vie de Jésus,* p. 502.
[3] Blessed Angela of Foligno.

2. INTERIOR PURITY.

(a) Silence.

"This is the reason," says the *Imitation,* "why there are found so few contemplative persons: because there are few that wholly sequester themselves from transitory and created things . . . . It is a great impediment that we so much regard signs and sensible things, and have but little of perfect mortification." [4]

Silence is necessary for us. Our Lady's life was silent. There was not much talking at Nazareth. If one wants to live a perfect Christian life, one must avoid unnecessary amusements, empty reading, idle protracted conversations, such as are not justified by charity or politeness. "To converse with others more than is really necessary and reason demands," says St. John of the Cross, "never did anyone any good, however holy he might be."

This exterior silence is not enough. Interior recollection is far more necessary. What is the good of being silent if inner voices are raised in loud clamor? God is ever giving Himself to us, the Holy Spirit is ever imparting supernatural inspirations, making so to say private revelations which show us our vocation more clearly every day: lights for our intelligence, strength for our will. A recollected soul grasps these inspirations. A soul is near holiness when recollection has made it so sensitive and prompt that it perceives and follows these inspirations. Because of their

---

[4] Book III, ch. 31.

interior dissipation, some souls do not even recognize their special vocation, to say nothing of living up to it. "My soul is continually in my hands," said the Psalmist, "and I have not forgotten Thy law" (Ps. cxviii, 109).

Our Lady preserved silence without, recollection within. Her life was a long silence. She watched her Son attentively and with reverent wonder. She listened to Him. She meditated on the mysteries before her eyes. St. Luke tells us (ii, 19) that "Mary kept all these words, pondering them in her heart," conferring thus with God about the mysteries of her Son: in those interior colloquies she saw ever more clearly His vocation and her own, the thoughts and intentions of God about the salvation of the world.

(b) Renunciation.

In order to prepare us for prayer, Our Lady gives us a taste for the inner purity which is an approach to her own special grace, perfect purity. Self-renunciation is the beginning of it. "If any man will come after me, let him deny himself," said Jesus (Luke ix, 23). The more we try to go to God, the better we understand the immense bearing of that saying of the Lord. We must relinquish ourselves, or, more simply, we must forget ourselves, and seek God alone. We must come to be able to say, like St. Paul: "I live, now not I but Christ liveth in me" (Gal. ii, 20).

What must we do for that?

We must in one word simplify our outlook. In our

mind: we must see all that happens, and our neighbor, only
in the light of God.   In our will, we must have one single
purpose, to work for the accomplishment of the divine will.
In our heart, we must be animated by the spirit of Christ,
as St. Paul tells us (I Cor. ii, 16).   In our emotions, we
must check the vagaries of the imagination which scatter
our inmost energies, we must banish anxiety about the
future, memories of the past.   In our daily life: we must
renounce our tastes, our love of comfort, we must overcome our repugnances, practice mortification in food, in
furniture, and never seek our personal gratification, for "they
that are Christ's have crucified their flesh" (Gal. ii, 24).
Even in our outward conduct: we must follow the motions
of grace, without evasion or cavilling when the duties of
our state and of charity impel us; we must do our duty with
courage, and trust afterwards to the providence of God.

Such a soul tends to live the words of Christ: "Seek first
the kingdom of God and His justice" (Matt. vi, 33).   Its
deepest tendency is obediently to follow the divine motions
and to keep always in contact with God.   It longs to be
able to say with St. Paul: "I have suffered the loss of all
things, and count them but as dung, that I may gain Christ"
(Phil. iii, 8).

God indeed is not slow to give Himself to a soul that,
following Our Lady, has renounced itself.   "Think of Me,"
said Jesus to Catherine of Siena, "and I will think of thee."

The soul has simply to forget itself, to surrender itself: God will do the rest, His purifying action will be exercised on it and it will be filled with divine life.

II. Our Lady Teaches Us to Pray in Joy.

1. MARY'S JOYS.

Although sorrow had a great place in the mysteries of the childhood of Jesus, yet they were marked by intense joys.   It would be impossible to express what Our Lady felt when, in the cave at Bethlehem, she saw Jesus for the first time.   From the first moment that she carried Him in her womb she had adored Him in silence.   Now she saw Him, her child and her God!   At her first sight of her Son she was filled with unspeakable love and adoration.   Mary's whole being spoke in the eyes, humble, tender, luminous, which she turned on her Son, knowing that in Him she was looking at the human face of God.

What a state she saw Him in!   Helpless, like all children. In greater indigence than other children.   But she blessed the helplessness and the indigence which would oblige her continually to intervene in His life and to show her love in all kinds of ways as mothers do for their little ones.   It was her happiness eagerly to perform the offices of a mother. She would take Him in her arms, wrap Him in swaddling clothes, smile at Him, caress Him with respect and deep adoration. What joy there was for the Blessed Virgin in that humble, tender, burning love which filled her being!

He was her God and she adored Him. He was her Son and she loved Him.

Jesus responded with divine magnificence. Between them there was an interchange of tenderness, love, life—an unceasing mutual giving. Mary was capable of receiving everything that Jesus was pleased to give to His mother and she responded fully. She was "pure capacity for Jesus, filled with Jesus." She was wholly a mother, she referred everything to Him, it was her nature to belong entirely to Him and to please Him. "The heart of each lived and breathed only through the other. How can we conceive the degree of loving union and the mutual influence each on each of those two hearts, so close and so divine, and living together such a lofty life?" . . . . "It is a mystery of the heart," adds Bèrulle, "and no tongue can express that sweetness and that mutual affection." [5]

This intimacy was the spring of limitless joys for Mary. She was happy in being what she was to Jesus: in belonging to Him wholly; in having received so many graces which would enable Him to offer her as an admirable gift to His Father, the gift to purchase which He would shed His blood. She was happy in being so intimately associated with His work and having to glorify God by a life and a sacrifice in common.

And so it was all along her ministry with regard to Jesus.

---

[5] Cardinal de Bérulle, *Ouevres,* p. 1002.

She ever surrounded her Son's humanity with love and solicitude. She was ever offering Him to His Father. It was her first act after His birth at Bethlehem, which she renewed so often, and especially in tragic fashion in the Temple on the day of the Presentation. At Nazareth they lived together, praying together, working side by side. If Christ's apostolic life sometimes brought about a separation, it was a purely external separation, during which Mary remained united in heart with her Son, followed Him in His mission, adored the manifestations of His divinity. Each of her Son's acts was a source of love for her mother's heart.

Besides, was she not His collaborator in the work of redemption? She was a sharer in His mysteries. Her motherhood made everything common to them.

2. OUR JOYS.

This part of Our Lady's life is fruitful for our own inner life. It ordinarily happens that the Lord fills beginners in the spiritual life with joy. Is it the reward of their conversion? Is it a preparation for the trials to come? Both, no doubt. "I am convinced that these graces are intended to strengthen our weakness and to make us capable, by the example of Jesus, of bearing great sufferings," says St. Teresa.[6] They are favors of the divine goodness which, if properly accepted, will produce precious effects.

Usually, they detach us from material things, and give

[6] *The Interior Castle.*

us courage to serve God, to whom they attract us as to the source of true happiness. Sometimes the heart is flooded with sensible sweetness before the tabernacle, after reading a page of the Gospel, after meditation. Or there comes what St. Thomas describes, "a certain spiritual delight which accompanies perfect acts of the virtues," after an act of self-sacrifice, or when a temptation is overcome. Or one experiences a lively sense of love of God, profound quietude, peace of soul grounded in friendship with God. These joys, far different from sensible pleasures, are a delight to the heart; they help one mightily to attach oneself wholly to Christ. They are a source of light. How many of us have begun, in such blessed moments, to understand God's greatness, His Goodness, the malice of sin, and to shed abundant tears for our wretched past! Our will gets new strength from them. The Christian rests in the sense of God's sweetness and mercy. In the desire of eternal things his soul thrills and expands. St. Bruno who was so calm and gentle sometimes walked about the Chartreuse mountain crying out: "O the goodness of God! the goodness of God!"

3. OUR LADY SHOWS US HOW TO TAKE THESE JOYS.

It is important to receive these favors with the necessary dispositions. "If anyone were to imagine," said St. Teresa, "that God's purpose was merely to make us enjoy His caresses, it would be a great mistake." [7]   Our Lady shows

---
[7] *Ibid.*

us how to receive God's blessings: with thanksgiving and humility. "My spirit hath rejoiced in God my Saviour because He hath regarded the lowliness of His handmaid."

Nothing would be more fatal than any thought of pride. These joys must not prevent us from seeing our faults. God is good to us; but He stoops to our wretchedness. A man is inclined to think himself better when he is happy. If a soul gets some light about the Godhead, the tendency is, alas, to think that by that fact it grows more acceptable to God, whereas it has only received an alms. It is not the liveliness of its feelings that shows the value of a soul, but its resolution to serve God at any cost. Very often, when God gives us these consolations, it is because He sees our weakness; and He treats us like children. At the beginning of our spiritual life, He takes us as we are, very close to earth, with imperfect inclinations; and he tries to win us by showing us the happiness of the spiritual life and making us lose our taste for other pleasures. "Mind the things that are above," says St. Paul, "not the things that are upon the earth" (Col. iii, 2). Spiritualize your devotion, and do not desire to pray with sighs, but make acts of will, interior acts.

Besides, keep silent always about these divine favors. What an indiscretion it is to talk about them! See how Mary kept God's secret. Gabriel told her that she would be the mother of the Messiah: she said nothing, even to Joseph. She waited for God Himself to reveal the unheard-of favor: "It is good to hide the secret of a King" (Tob. xii, 7). The Blessed Virgin loved the silence that God alone penetrates, "pondering in her heart" on all that she had seen and heard (Luke ii, 19.)

4. OUR LADY UNITES US WITH THE JOY OF JESUS AND HER OWN.

(a) The joy of adoration.

God created His children for joy.

Jesus wants us to live in joy; He asked it of His Father on the eve of His death: Holy Father, I pray "that they may have My joy filled in themselves" (John xvii, 13).

The joy of Jesus, His sovereign joy which dominated all else, was the contemplation of His Father, the sight of His divine perfection. God exists, essential being, goodness, love, beauty, sovereign purity! And the soul of Jesus contemplated Him in His essence, unveiled. The joy of that contemplation was the supreme point of His interior life. It was the fulness of His joy,[8] a joy that nothing, not even the terrible Passion, could spoil, an invulnerable joy.

It was Mary's joy too. It must be ours. The Church perpetually invites us to it; in the Mass she asks us to praise

---

[8] "Ask and you shall receive, that your joy may be full" (John xvi, 24).

the Lord, to adore Him, to glorify Him, to give Him thanks. Why? "For His great glory," because He is infinitely happy in His Son. Let us praise the infinite perfection of God, let us praise His happiness. Let us praise Him in His love—the love that He bears to Himself, in His Spirit—and the love that He bears to creatures.

(b) The joy of glorification.

Joy will come to us also, as to Our Lady, from the contemplation of Jesus. Let our praises break forth in thanksgiving for the incarnation of the Word, who became our brother; in deep wonder at the divine greatness that has stooped so low: "He emptied Himself . . . . He loved me and delivered Himself for me" (Phil. ii, 7; Gal. ii, 20).

Above all, let us rejoice because the incarnation of the Word gave God sovereign glory. Jesus is the perfect adorer of the Father who gives that adoration in spirit and in truth. He makes reparation, He is the penitent who plunges into an abyss of shame in order to restore God's creation to Him. His Passion was to inaugurate the reign of God on earth.

As Mary lived side by side with Her Son, it was for her an intense joy to know that the least acts of Jesus gave immense glory to God; and she joined with all her heart in that glorification.

Let us unite our thoughts with theirs. Nothing lifts up

the soul like this religious reverence for God. It is one of
the most attractive and beneficent forms of love. This preoccupation with the glory of God shows that we really
belong to the family of God. "Jesus is happy: I lack
nothing," said Père de Foucauld in his desert.

(c) The joy of gratitude.

Let us rejoice to belong to God, to be united with Him
in grace. Even in the most terrible sufferings, Our Lady
preserved unalterable joy because she was God's, because
she never knew sin, and because love was in her. And
where there is love, there is joy. "O eternal God," said
St. Catherine of Siena, "Thou art a tranquil ocean in which
souls live and feed. They find their rest there in the union
of love."

The thought of the presence of God should produce
intense joy in us. Every increase of grace is a communication from God, a new contact with God. In comparison
with that, the thought of suffering would be a little thing.
When one of the seven swords of Mary's sorrows pierced
her heart, the thought of the limitless graces that would
flow from it for her and of the glory it would give to God
made the sorrow produce joy in her heart and increased
her love.

Christ felt boundless joy at the thought of the Passion

and of the glory that would redound to God from His terrible sufferings. "I have a baptism wherewith I am to be baptized, and how am I straitened until it be accomplished" (Luke xii, 50). His Passion was the triumph of His love, of His gratitude. His humanity had received everything from the Father, the infinite glory of the hypostatic union; what return could It make? That is why He delivered Himself up to the Passion, and went through it "unto the end" (John xiii, 1). Through love of His Father: "that the world may know that I love the Father" (John xiv, 31). Suffering, in a sense, relieved Him; it enabled His love to pay its debt, at the same time as the debt of men.

God's consolations should produce that disposition in us. In Christ love carried it to the point of sacrifice. So also in the Christian. "To suffer and to be despised," said St. John of the Cross.

Sometimes it will be easy to perform these acts of praise, thanksgiving, reverent wonder. At other times not. The prayer of praise is not always borne upwards by intense sensible emotion. There are moments when the feelings of the heart cannot rise to the lips. We must then remember that fidelity is the real proof of love. Instead of offering vague feelings, offer your labors, your sufferings.

Above all, offer Jesus, as Our Lady so often did. In the Temple she offered Him with unexampled love and unselfishness, offering herself along with her Son, becoming a victim with Him. Through Mary, offer the praise, adoration, labors, sufferings of Jesus to the Father. Offer His unique love. Offer His blood. Unite with the present sentiments of Christ in heaven, where He leads the prototypal liturgy before the throne of God. Let it be through Him that we "offer God the sacrifice of praise" (Ps. xlix, 14). We are nothing, our works are of no value, but Jesus allows us to use Him: His blood is of infinite value, and He shed it for the glory of God.

Look on Thy Son, O my God, on Him who is Thy eternal blessedness. I offer Him to Thee, to express our praise, our adoration, our thanksgiving. "Through Him and with Him and in Him be to Thee, Father Almighty, in the unity of the Holy Ghost all honor and glory for ever and ever."

It is hard to describe the benefits of this prayer of praise and reverent wonder. The joy that the soul finds in it increases its love, a love of delight which rapidly becomes a love of conformity. "My Lord, teach me what Thou willest me to say to Thee," cried St. Margaret Mary. "Nothing," answered Jesus, "but: 'my God, my only love and my all; Thou art all to me, and I am entirely Thine.' "

It is a great grace to be able in prayer first of all to see God. That is how the saints pray. As for us, too often we think of ourselves. The saints began by adoring, revering,

praising.   Their prayer was a canticle, a spontaneous up-
lifting of the heart to the divine majesty.   They felt impelled
to extol God.

This prayer of praise makes us live in love.   Make many
acts of love: "Abide in My love," said Our Lord (John xv,
19).   Tell God that you love Him.   Tell it to Him constantly—apropos of the graces you have received, of the
trials you have borne or will bear, of your joys and your
sufferings.   Love Him for yourself, and for all others.   Love
Him by praising Him, adoring Him, obeying Him, surrendering yourself unreservedly to His will.

III.   Our Lady Teaches Us to Pray in Faith.

1. JESUS GOES AWAY.

The joyful mysteries fill only a part of the life of Jesus
and Mary.   The interior life is a bitter struggle in a valley
of tears.   We must expect suffering.   After a meditation
full of joy in which God visibly speaks to us, there will
come a depressing period when God seems to draw away:
Jesus is silent and goes from us.   It is a formidable time.

Our Lady's life gives us an example of that.   She went
through days of real agony when Jesus stayed behind in
the Temple without telling her.   Jesus gone, gone without
a word!   He had said nothing and had left her.   It seemed
to her that she no longer understood Him.   That, her inner

torture, was her worst suffering. Why had her Son abandoned her? Could God the Father have recalled Him and was that the sword of sorrow foretold by Simeon?

When she found Him, His answer appeared harsh: "How is it that you sought Me? Did you not know that I must be about My Father's business?" (Luke ii, 49). Yes, she knew it. But she did not think that her Son would busy Himself about God's glory without her. She said nothing, she did not understand, but she felt cruel anguish and went through a mysterious trial. Was she repulsed by God and by her Son?

Such trials are necessary for us. Through faith it is that we advance towards God. We must not hope that we shall continue to feel Jesus near in all our exercises of piety, that we shall sensibly enjoy His presence in communion, and that grace will continue to support us almost visibly. From us also, one day, Jesus goes. And the whole of our life is changed. The divine intimacy ceases. Prayer grows tiresome. Communion seems to produce no result. The tabernacle is empty. Penance is repugnant and discouraging. Formerly, I was drawn to divine things: now, I do not even feel the desire of God. Everything pulls me down. In the past my heart burned as I ran forward eagerly towards God; now I lag, my spirit is cold, not an act of love rises from my unfeeling heart.

Such moments are decisive in the spiritual life. The soul is at an important turning-point. It is essential to keep united in heart with the Blessed Virgin Mary.

We must first notice in Mary's case that when Jesus went from her, the Holy Ghost continued to sanctify her, and that those three days of anguish lifted her to an immense height. Sometimes it is the same with us. But we must not forget that what is called spiritual dryness may be a punishment inflicted by God's mercy. We can lose Jesus through our own fault. The just sometimes lose Jesus for their perfecting. Sinners lose Him because they have driven Him away. Others lose Him because, though their love is not dead, it has slackened and grown tepid. You must first humble yourself: has not Jesus left you because of your pride, your self-complacency, your cowardice about penance, your dissipation, your looking for human consolation and sensible friendship, your rejection of grace? It is hard to judge whence the absence of Jesus comes: almost always we are to some extent at fault. God wants our whole heart. But these punishments that God's mercy inflicts on our luke-warmness are a sign of His great love for our souls and a mark of our vocation to holiness.

"Learn from Mary to see Jesus," says Origen. We must not remain inactive in that state, nor resign ourselves to God's absence. Our Lady desired ardently to find Jesus: she sought Him until she found Him.

But it is He alone that we must seek.   How sad it is if
in these moments we commit the indelicacy of seeking consolation from creatures!   There is only one consolation: to
find Him again.   Let us seek Him where He is: in penance,
in works of charity, in the Gospel, in prayer, in the Eucharist.
You will never find Him in pleasures, even innocent
pleasures; and rarely amongst your friends.

Be ready to seek Him long, if it seems good to Him;
and not to recover along with Him the consolations He
gave you at the beginning of your spiritual life.   Consolations, even divine ones, are not God.   Set your heart above
all on the divine life.

2. THE PRAYER OF FAITH.

But it does happen that dryness is a trial.   God seems
to withdraw from the soul in order to train it in detachment, truer humility, trust.   He wants to detach it from
everything sensible, and from everything that flatters self-
love.   The very favors that God gives us at the beginning
of our interior life necessitate this purification; for nature
steps in, and what God gives us holily we receive with
more or less impurity.[9]

It is an inevitable trial.   Fervent souls will necessarily
go through this purification, for in our relations with God

---

[9] M. Olier.

we must substitute supernatural activity for natural activity, that is, we must develop the function of the theological virtues.

In those moments of semi-blindness, we must accustom ourselves to see Jesus in faith: hearing nothing, feeling nothing, not hoping for an answer. To urge us to pray then, there is only faith, which knows that God, God who is silent, is yet there, adorable and lovable.

St. Teresa of Lisieux long knew that trial. She thought of Mary: "I never so well understood," she says, "the bitter pain of the Blessed Virgin and St. Joseph seeking the divine Child Jesus in the streets of Jerusalem. I was in a fearful desert." [10]

Prayer in these circumstances is grievous. The mind is powerless, as if struck with paralysis. Beforehand, we were recollected, spiritual reading moved us, drew us towards God. Now, we think, is the moment to pray. We try, and it all vanishes. All the fruit of our previous reading is gone. So true it is that contemplation does not come from the activity of the intelligence, but from purity, freedom from the senses, love.

Sometimes the trial is worse. Those truths that we meditated on with so much joy we no longer understand. Faith seems to have evaporated. "Then," says St. Teresa, "faith

---

[10] *Histoire d'une âme, ch. V.*

is deadened and, as it were, plunged in sleep along with the other virtues. It is not dead, for one continues to believe what the Church teaches. But it is as if the mouth alone pronounced the formula. On the other hand one's heart is numb, one is in a strange lethargy. In this state, what the soul retains of knowledge of God is like a vague sound heard afar off. When He is spoken of, it accepts what is said as a thing admitted because the Church teaches it, but it has no memory whatever of its own experiences."

The heart is dry. "In a desert land, and where there is no way and no water, so in the sanctuary have I come before Thee to see Thy power and Thy glory" (Ps. lxii, 3). The flame of the heart is burnt out. Prayer is tiring and boring. Yet the soul endeavors to pray. Its prayer is dry, turns often on a few formulas: "Lord, Thou art holy, I adore Thee . . . . Lord, Thou art infinite love, I wish I could love Thee, help me to love Thee . . . . Lord, I believe that Thou art present here, I wish I could serve Thee, glorify Thee, but I do not know how to do it. Take me into Thy service, purify me from my sins, do with me what Thou willest."

In fact, the will of this soul is turned to God. It feels no tenderness, as it used to do, but it has without suspecting it a calm love, capable of enduring everything for God.

3. Following Our Lady.

Here we must imitate Our Lady's dispositions, especially

her resignation. Jesus often had to go away from her, apart from the three days' separation in the Temple. He left her to undertake His apostolic life. And when one day she stood outside waiting to see Him, "one said unto Him: Behold Thy Mother and Thy brethren stand without, seeking Thee. But He answering . . . said: Who is My Mother? . . . . Whosoever shall do the will of My Father" (Matt. xii, 47-50). The words seem harsh to a mother's heart. Each time that Jesus speaks publicly of His Mother, His beloved Mother, it is to bruise her heart of flesh, to shatter so to say her sensible affection, pure though it was, and to direct it along the path of purely spiritual love. As Co-Redemptress, she had to resemble the Redeemer; her love had like His to be a thing apart.

Similarly, we must accustom ourselves to the sensible absence of Jesus, to His apparent harshness; we must live in faith. "I thank Jesus," said St. Teresa of Lisieux, "for making me walk in darkness; I am in deep peace. I willingly consent to spend all my religious life in that dark cellar into which He has brought me. I desire only that my darkness should win light for sinners." After having lived for many years in that state, she said at the moment of death: "I do not regret having surrendered myself to love."

Let us remain at peace. It is not a good sign for a soul to indulge in complaints about this aridity. At such moments faith is the only refuge, and, moreover, it is the most profit-able. "No insight into supernatural things could help us so much, to grow in the love of God, as the least act of living faith and hope performed in complete deprivation of light." [11]

Let us seek Him then in faith and in persevering desire. If your mind is stricken with a sort of paralysis, your heart numbed, you still have the fundamental aspiration of faith turned entirely to God; you still have the grief of not loving, as you would like to love, Him who is infinitely lovable. You can always desire to serve Him, to love Him: that desire is in itself service and love.

4. Prayer in the Night.

But even this prayer in faith needs to be purified.

We must still follow Our Lady. Was she not the mother of a son destitute of the necessaries of life, unrecognized, exiled, calumniated, condemned? The desolation of Calvary! She climbed that hill in the midst of a crowd that shrieked out its hatred. Her Son was suffering fearfully, and why? Those men seemed not to want to be saved. It was complete failure. Even the apostles had fled. Had the might of God suffered an eclipse? She heard that most mysterious cry of

---

[11] St. John of the Cross.

her Son from the depth of the abyss: "My God, My God, why has Thou forsaken Me?" (Matt. xxvii, 46).

Our Lady takes the soul that wants to follow her into the abyss of her desolation, into Christ's desolation.

That soul gets into a strange state. It experiences sudden crushing surprises, it falls a victim to scruples, to agonizing anxiety; even at prayer, the demon assails it with fierce temptations, and it ends by believing that it is far from God, that it is following an evil path and will be lost.

Hitherto it had endured great sufferings from without: it had been blamed and persecuted by the world, profoundly shaken by illness, disappointed on all sides. But it had turned towards God and found relief in saying to Him: "It is for Thee, my God."

Even now it turns towards God. But He is not there. Has the God of purity taken an aversion to it? The soul feels disgust for itself. It is like the agony of Jesus: Jesus had taken our sins on Himself, and pursued sin relentlessly in His humanity. Mary followed Him because of her spiritual motherhood, and did not desire to spare herself any more than He; she, the Immaculate, had also taken on herself and was expiating the sins of her children. And now infinite purity fixes its gaze so to say on the soul led by Mary; It searches it out in its deepest recesses; a light shines into its most tortuous windings and reveals its most hidden secrets. The soul thought itself pure! It thought that it loved God! But infinite purity shows it its impurity. How can it venture henceforth to turn to God? Yet, only His mercy can purify it. It tries to pray, it invokes mercy and love, it protests that it desires to love. But where is God, God for whom after all one's whole being is broken in agony? He does not answer. Is He weary of the soul? And yet it is for Him that it is enduring such suffering. For Him the soul longs. But the very consolation that sprang from suffering vanishes; what in suffering seemed lovely, divine, has disappeared. One has to bear the pain with no spontaneity, with distaste, alone; and why? One even asks oneself whether this very pain is not an offense against God. "My God, My God, why has Thou forsaken me?"

The suffering of the soul in this desolation is indescribable. "The greatest torment of the soul," says St. John of the Cross, "is to think that God hates it, abandons it, and therefore casts it into darkness."[12] "Listen to the martydom that thou shalt have to suffer," said Our Lady to St. Veronica. "Thou wilt love, yet be convinced that thou knowest not love. Thou wilt love to the point of torment, yet be persuaded that thou art betraying love. People will speak to thee of love, and thou wilt seem to hear a foreign language.

---

[12] *Dark Night of the Soul,* Book II, ch. 6.

And thy torment will be the impossibility of understanding and expressing thy torment." [13]

What is Our Lady's purpose? To purify this member of Christ, to lead him to absolute self-renunciation, by depriving him of everything that consoled and supported him. It is good to love the Cross and to desire to save the world with Christ: but it is a positive breach of order to find satisfaction in that thought. It is the destruction of suffering if it is spoiled by that canker-worm. It is good for the Christian to experience the nothingness of all things, as St. John of the Cross says, and to feel disgust for himself. It brings humility, true convinced humility, such humility as opens the way for the full play of grace. "The soul is then so humiliated and made so pliable by the difficulties, temptations, tribulations of every kind through which God is training it, that it becomes gentler and more tractable in its relations with Him, with itself, and with the neighbor." [14]

In reality, it is the Holy Ghost working in the soul, as in Our Lady during the days of the Passion which were the occasion of terrible suffering and of immense sanctification. A great union is established between Jesus and the soul which has entered into the mystery of the Passion.

---

[13] Désiré des Planches, *Le journal de sainte Véronique Giuliani,* p. 75. Paris, 1931.

[14] St. John of the Cross, *Dark Night of the Soul,* Book I, ch. 13.

Blessed Angela of Foligno lived through those painful hours: "It was impossible to praise God, impossible to pray. I saw nothing divine left in me but the absolute will not to sin . . . . At last God took pity, and I heard these words: 'O my daughter and my beloved, the love of God rests in thee.'

"And my soul cried:

" 'How shall I believe Thee, from the depths of my abyss, when I feel myself abandoned?'

"He replied:

" 'The more thou thinkest thyself abandoned, the more thou art loved and held close by God . . . . Know that in this state God and thou are more intimately united than ever'." [15]

CHAPTER VI.

Our Lady Defends Our Spiritual Life.

I. Against the Devil.

II. Against Creatures.

III. Against Ourselves.

IV. Mother of Mercy.

I. Against the Devil.

Temptation is a universal fact. None of us can hope to escape that mysterious law. It is even certain that souls called to perfection are more violently tempted; being more loved by God they excite more bitter jealousy in the enemy of the human race; being more powerful through their choice graces, they have the possibility of snatching many of his followers from the devil. Moreover, the fall of such chosen souls is a loss to the Kingdom of God, and that alone would explain the number and violence of the temptations that assail them.

Our Lady defends her children.

Is not she, the Immaculate, the great adversary of Satan? She has the mandate to crush his head. Her absolute purity gives her an unspeakable horror of everything that leads to sin.

As the mother of Jesus, she wants to defend Him in us. When the devil assails our supernatural life, it is in fact Jesus Himself that he is assailing. What he wants to extinguish in us is the life of Christ. Do you not understand that the mother of Jesus is moved to the very depths of her being, and eager to defend her Son's honor? For the honor of God is at stake in us. We are children of God, co-heirs with Christ, temples of the Holy Ghost. This living reality excites the bitter hatred of the devil. It is still Christ that he persecutes in us and would like to crucify again. "If the world," which is actuated by the devil, "hate you," said Christ, "know ye that it hath hated Me before you" (John vx, 18).

That is also the source of our strength. We are associated with Christ's personal cause, and all that is His rallies to our defense: Mary in the first place who regards as done to her Son what is done to His members.

The mystery of the Incarnation is the perpetual motive of conflict between the devil and men. That is why Our Lady takes a direct part in that terrible struggle.

She did not become our mother in such terrible suffering to abandon us to the enemy of God. She provides us with grace as the principle of our resistance, an active and inexhaustible principle which she adapts to our temptations and weaknesses. We know that with that grace—sometimes our refuge, sometimes our strength — no power is capable of snatching a soul from God: "Who shall separate us from the love of Christ? Shall tribulation? Or distress? Or famine? Or nakedness? Or danger? Or persecution? Or the sword? . . . . In all these things we overcome, because of Him that hath loved us. For I am sure that neither death, nor life, nor angels, nor principalities, nor powers, nor things present, nor things to come, nor might, nor height, nor depth, nor any other creature shall be able to separate us from the love of God, which is in Christ Jesus Our Lord" (Rom. viii, 35-39).

Has not Our Lady the angels at her service? "There are more with us than with them" (IV Kings vi, 16), said Eliseus to his servant who was frightened by a pursuing crowd. And at the Prophet's prayer the servant saw Mount Carmel covered with celestial horsemen. So does Our Lady place heaven at our service. She is Queen of Angels: it is not an empty title. She often directs her children on earth by means of angels, especially when it is a case of fighting the devils.

As grace is the source of joy, Our Lady enables us to combat temptation by joy. The spirit of joy is a very great strength against temptation. For when all is said and done, joy is love, it is the soul dilating in the possession of God.

"In Thy strength, O Lord, the king shall joy and in Thy salvation he shall rejoice exceedingly," says David (Ps. xx, 2). So much so that the simplest way to triumph over temptation is not to grow agitated, not to discuss the wiles of the tempter, but to cling with all our will to Him who lives in us and who, more than we ourselves, wants to save the life that He imparts to us. "As therefore you have received Jesus Christ the Lord, walk ye in Him; rooted and built up in Him and confirmed in the faith" (Col. ii, 67).

Temptation itself becomes a source of joy. It is a battle fought and won for the kingdom of God; and you have the joys of victory. Hence St. James said: "Count it all joy when you shall fall into divers temptations" (i, 2).

II. Against Creatures.

Often also creatures are an obstacle to our Christian life. Not rarely they oppose the accomplishment of the will of God: sometimes unintentionally, sometimes quite consciously.

Our Lady suffered much from that. Her life is full of instances of the opposition of creatures: the indifference of the people of Bethlehem compelled her to give birth to her Child in a cave; Herod's hatred made her flee in terror; her fellow townsmen in Nazareth tried to throw her Son down from the brow of the hill; the Pharisees, the ancients, and very many others, pursuing her Son with their hostility even to death, caused her hours of anguish.

So that Our Lady understands the opposition of creatures to the work of God. Think of how they received her Son, of the torment of her heart when she saw the Creator, made man through love, not only rejected by His people, but actually detested and pursued with unrelenting hatred.

How did Our Lady answer? Always in the same way, with her mother's love. She loved those men who detested Jesus, she would have suffered any torture to destroy their hatred, to show them Jesus. For them, too, she delivered up her Son to Calvary. She wanted to save them.

It is a lesson of love. Our Lady teaches us a difficult thing, to consent to suffer through our neighbor. When suffering comes to us direct from God, we accept it ordinarily enough: the Church has so often told us that we must carry our cross with Christ that we take it patiently. The difficulty is greater when the cross is presented to us by our neighbor. We do not like our neighbor to come between God and us. We bear it when God strikes us, but not when He strikes us through men. Rare are the Christians who have enough faith, and especially enough humility, to recognize God's hand in the neighbor's. In the misfortunes which come to us direct from men, even the most religious people often see only evidence of bad temper, mean display of jealousy, unjust suspicions, ingratitude, and even malice. Who can see the justice and love of God using a creature for the good of His children? It is in that that we discover the true humility of the servants of God, so profound is our repugnance to suffering through the neighbor. Only the humble accept it. One must almost have reached holiness to understand that the neighbor takes the place of God in our purification.

Sometimes the trial is worse still. Not only do the enemies of God cross your path, but good men rise up against you: cruel defections, lack of understanding, harsh interpretation of your actions, public blame, your zeal stigmatized as harmful, your plans opposed as being dangerous. "One of the greatest sufferings of this exile," said St. Peter of Alcantara to St. Teresa, "is the opposition of good people." Did not the five theologians deputed to examine St. Teresa's manuscripts declare, all five, that what she wrote came from the devil, and thus plunge her into fearful anxiety? How many bishops interdicted St. Louis Mary Grignion de Montfort, Mary's great apostle? St. Alphonsus de'Liguori was driven out of the congregation he had founded. Do not imagine that such trials are very rare. How many of the faithful and how many priests, after having devotedly organized some work, are put aside on the ground of having lost its spirit! How many apostles there are whose intentions are calumniated every day!

A glance at Our Lady reassures them. She also walked by

that road. Was she not the mother of one who was rejected, calumniated, hunted down by the doctors of the law and the chief priests? Still worse, did not that beloved Son leave her, when He was twelve, when He was thirty; did He not treat her with apparent indifference: "Who is my mother? . . . .Whosoever shall do the will of God, he is my brother and my sister and mother" (Mark iii, 33-35).

What Jesus sought was to lead his mother to the most utter detachment of spiritual poverty. He Himself was absolutely poor. His material poverty was great, still greater His spiritual poverty. He lived detached from all things, and died abandoned by His disciples, rejected by His people, dishonored by a public condemnation, without His power which suffered eclipse, and even without human form, disfigured by His tortures.

So does He will to live in His mystical body. His members must live by the beatitudes, by love of poverty, meekness, mercy, in persecutions, abandonment to Providence, detachment from all things and from life itself. "As having nothing," says St. Paul, "and possessing all things" (II Cor. vi, 10). Selfless, spiritually poor, they already "possess the kingdom of God" (I Cor. vi. 10).

Opposition on the part of creatures is permitted by God to purify the zeal and love of His members. We tend all too much to mingle personal preoccupations with our desire of glorifying God. The opposition of creatures helps us to sanctify ourselves.

Creatures inflict a still deeper suffering on the servant of God. That was perhaps the most terrible that Our Lady experienced. She began to endure it at the Presentation. She offered her Son for the salvation of the world. Surely men will rush to the arms of the Saviour? Simeon answers: "This child is set for the fall . . . . of many" (Luke ii, 35). Jesus, who is beauty and love, an occasion of fall! He came to save us but He was not accepted: "His own received Him not" (John i, 11). What a terrible surprise for His mother's heart! It lasted all her life; the priests had no use for the Christ; the crowd were deceived; and even at the last hour so was that impenitent thief for whom Mary was praying and who nevertheless died blaspheming. To die close to the cross of salvation, side by side with God the Redeemer, and to be lost! Were the sufferings of Jesus in vain?

Who could describe the pain of the apostles in face of the obstinacy of men? The servants of God too, driven by thirst for souls, persist in preaching the love of the Saviour; they spend their lives in that; contemplatives pray; penitents sacrifice themselves. Yet there are moments when they see nothing but the innumerable procession of unbelievers and of the baptised moving towards the abyss of hell. Is the apostolate, is prayer, in vain?

Yet they regret nothing, any more than Our Our Lady at the foot of the Cross, who did not regret a single pang or torment or drop of blood. For in these things she saw the glory of God, and souls.

What does Our Lady seek? To get us to throw ourselves on God. To make us acknowledge God everywhere and love Him everywhere, especially in our neighbor who serves His sovereign will. "This is the will of God, your sanctification" (I Thess. iv, 3), says St. Paul. God aims only at that because all His designs are bound up with the great mystery of Christ, with the formation of the mystical Christ, whose mother Mary is. Because she coöperates with God in that formation of the saints, she persuades me that when God wills me to be humbled and contradicted by my neighbor, His will is inspired by a father's love.

III. Against Ourselves.

Alas, the devil and creatures are not the most dangerous adversaries of our Christian life. We are ourselves more dangerous because we are sinners and inclined to sin. And here it is perhaps that Our Lady's goodness makes itself most strongly felt.

God has an inexpressible hatred for sin. Think of the agony of Jesus. Our Lady had an extremely deep super-natural knowledge of sin. Her lofty faith showed her its horror. Her holiness and her Immaculate Conception put her in radical opposition to it. On the day of the Passion, her spiritual motherhood plunged her into nameless grief.

What did she see? On the one hand her Son whom love of His Father and love of men led to deliver Himself up to suffering in order to blot out sin. He suffered in order to introduce us into the kingdom of love and to give the Church to His Father, purified of every stain, holy as a bride.

On the other hand she saw us, Christ's brethren, her own children, revealing as Simeon had foretold thoughts out of many hearts, and refusing to profit by His blood. She watched Jesus dying to save us, and yet foresaw that there would be lost souls among her children, her children whom she loved. She saw the obstinate sinner who rises up against the cross and endeavors to make the Redeemer's suffering of no avail.

I do not think that one can fathom the interior pain of Our Lady on Calvary. In face of infinite love, she was overwhelmed by the hideous, gigantic mass of the sins of the whole world, a mass of wickedness that rose up before God to insult and, as it were, to assault Him. And really that day it submerged her Son like a flood and plunged Him into anguish so horrible that He died uttering the mysterious cry: "My God, why hast Thou forsaken Me?"

And yet her love was not discouraged. She was a mother.

She shared the Passion to the end, going down to the very bottom of the abyss with her Son. She went to the limit of grief and love. As a mother, she had to try the impossible to save the children to whom she gave birth that day, even in spite of their rejection of infinite love.

It was at the foot of the Cross that she became the mother of mercy for all of us and that she acquired that formidable power against sin. May we feel that power! Deep detestation of sin is one of the first graces that Our Lady obtains for those who submit to her maternal influence. "If God were to let us choose which of the great and extraordinary gifts, that He has given to His Saints, should be conferred upon ourselves, we could not do better than ask for that piercing and overwhelming hatred of sin which some have had. It is a gift which lies at the root of all perfection, and is the supernatural vigor of all perseverance. It is at once the safest and the most operative of all singular graces. Devotion to Our Lady's dolors is a great help both to acquiring the hatred of sin as a habit, and to meriting it as a grace. The desolation wrought by sin in the heart of the sinless Mother . . . . fills us with horror, with pity, with indignation, with self-approach." [1]

To help us to enter into this feeling, Our Lady shows us her Son. That is her mission. She shows us the Lamb of

---

[1] Frederick Faber, *The Foot of the Cross,* p. 61, Ed. 1857.

God, her Son, penitent in a life of humiliation and toil, despised, seeking ignominy, "filled with contempt" (Ps. cxxii, 3), "a man of sorrows" (Is. liii, 3).

And that for my sins: "He was wounded for our iniquities, He was bruised for our sins (Is. liii, 5).

Blessed Angela of Foligno tells us that she asked from Our Lady whatever would be most pleasing to the Lord. Our Lady heard her prayer. "I was given compassion for Jesus and Mary," she says, "more efficacious than before. The biggest things that I did seemed little to me; and I conceived the desire of more exacting penances. My heart was enclosed in the Passion of Christ, and the hope of my salvation through that Passion was given me." The Saviour appeared to her crucified, showing His wounds, His scourging, His horrible pain. "He said: 'It is for thee that I suffered.' Then all my sins were present to my mind; I understood that I was perpetrator of the scourging. I understood what my sorrow ought to be. He kept on, showing me the course of His Passion, and saying: 'What wilt thou do to make a return to me'? I sobbed and wept, to such a degree that my tears burned my flesh." [2]

The memory of our sins and of the mercy which has forgiven us should keep sorrow constantly alive in us. Because Jesus had put on the likeness of sin (Rom. viii, 3), He lived

---

[2] Blessed Angela of Foligno, *Visions at révélations*, p. 49.   Hello.

in humiliation before His Father. The life of Mary, mother of the humiliated Christ, was spent in penance and sorrow. The saints feel that sorrow intensely. St. Vincent Ferrer, before entering the towns where he was preaching the gospel and performing miracles, would prostrate himself on the dusty roads and beg God with tears not to punish the place because of the sinner who was going into it.

Nothing is more important for our spiritual life than that constant sorrow for having committed sin. All our progress depends on it.

Not that we should be continually thinking of each of our past sins: prudance demands that we should forget them. But we must remember that we are sinners. The fact of having sinned, even if it were only once, should keep us ashamed. The spirit of Gethsemani should be over us. *Amplius lava me,* said David: "My God purify me still more" (Ps. 50). Let us think of the judgment that the incarnate Word passed on his pure humanity simply because it was laden with the sins of the world, and reflect that He submitted to the Cross. "There is no church service," wrote Ernest Psichari, "at which I do not shed abundant tears before the Master whom I so long crucified."

It is Mary who gives us the grace of this holy shame before God. "I am the mother of fair love, and of fear" (Ecclus. xxiv, 24), she says. "Penance! Penance!" she said at Lourdes.

At La Salette she appeared bathed in tears, weeping for our sins. It is she who leads us to humility, to true prayer, and creates in our soul the constant urge to make reparation, to love and glorify God.

IV. Mother of Mercy.

From the earliest times Christians gave that name to Our Lady, to indicate one of the essential qualities of her mother love. Mercy is compassion for the wretchedness of others. We have a high priest, says Holy Scripture (Hebr. ii, 17, 18) "merciful and faithful before God, that He might be a propitiation for the sins of the people. For in that, wherein He Himself hath suffered and been tempted, He is able to succor them also that are tempted." We have to say the same thing of the mother of our High Priest who shared suffering and trial with Him and whose heart is moved to solace our wretchedness.

Mercy is the most striking manifestation of the power and goodness of God. Power, when it is good, is what gives itself out most generously, and in most intimate ways. That alone would explain why Our Lady is so merciful: in that way she both takes pity on us and gives glory to God. St. Augustine tells us that it redounds more to God's glory to change a sinner into a just man than to have created the heavens and the earth: "Grace is a good of more value than the whole universe." Accordingly, one of the principal functions of Our Lady's maternity is the conversion of sinners.

Mary is mother of mercy because she gave us the Saviour, because she formed the humanity created to redeem us. The Redeemer is her great gift to us. "Amidst the terrors that beset me," said St. Anselm, "in the fear that paralyzes me, O most clement Queen, what mediatrix shall I invoke with more fervour than her whose womb bore the reconciliation of the world? What intercession will more easily win pardon for a criminal like me, than the prayer of her who fed with her milk the universal avenger of every crime and the merciful author of forgiveness?"

Our Lady is the true patroness of sinners. "She became mother of God," says Richard of St. Victor,[3] "for a purpose of mercy." Mercy flows inexhaustibly from her heart on sinners. Christians feel that deeply. In her presence the most wretched sinner, provided he desires to emerge from his filthiness, feels springing up in him a sense of trust, of security, as at his mother's feet. Christ gave her to us for forgiveness. Even on the days of our saddest lapses, we can continue to pray to her: "Pray for us sinners." However low unfortunate sinners fall, the memory of Mary remains like a life buoy to which they cling.

---

[3] Richard of St. Victor, *Explicatio in Cantica Canticorum*. J.-P. Migne, *Patrologia Latina*, CXCVI, 514-18.

The Church calls her: "Mirror of justice," of divine holiness; but also: "Refuge of sinners." Her mother-love inclines her to them; she sees on them the blood of her Son; she desires to make them one body with Jesus. Her mercy covers all Christ's members: the just, because they are in union with Him; sinners, so that they may be in union with Him.

We need only remember Calvary to have an idea of her unique mercy. How terrible her torture was! Love gave her over to Jesus, but also to the executioners. She was His mother and theirs. All those who were persecuting Jesus, the crowd clamoring for his death, shouting and crucifying Him, were her children! She had conceived them at the moment of the Incarnation, she gave them birth in her martyrdom; she had a mother's love for them, the love of a mother who loves always. "In her soul, which was more than crucified, it is impossible to discover the slightest trace of indignation, the faintest shadow of irritation. She does not appeal to the justice of God nor desire Him to take vengeance. If she invoked His justice it would be on herself. She sees everything but observes only one thing, namely, that Jesus her love is now surrendering Himself to that blessed justice, surrendering Himself with the meekness of a lamb. And she surrenders herself wholly, with Him and like Him. As for wishing any punishment whatever to the authors, in any capacity, of the crimes that are the cause, the occasion, and the setting of that great sacrifice, she has neither the urge nor the intention nor even the temptation to do so. That is not her function nor her character. Everywhere, all the time, but especially on Calvary, she is a woman, a mother; the clement Virgin, the advocate of sinners, the mother of mercy." [4]

Our Lady in heaven has that mercy in its supreme perfection. Her perpetual prayer is inspired by it. "Who could measure," says St. Bernard, "the length and the breadth, the height and the depth, of thy mercy, O Blessed Virgin? By its length it will help until the last day all those who implore it. By its breadth, that mercy fills the earth. Its height ascends to the city on high, to make good its losses. Its depth goes down to the lowest abysses, to set at liberty those who sit in darkness and the shadow of death; for by thee heaven has been filled, hell emptied, the ruins of the heavenly Jerusalem restored, Christian life given back to the wretched beings in whom sin had killed it." [5]

"I am the queen of heaven and the mother of mercy," said Our Lady to St. Bridget, "I am the joy of the just and the gate giving sinners access to God. There is no one, how-

[4] Msgr. C.-L. Gay, *Conférences aux mères chrétiennes,* 41e conf.

[5] St. Bernard, *In Assumptione B. Mariae Virginis Sermo IV*. J.-P. Migne, *Patrologia Latina.* CLXXXIII, 425-30.

ever accursed, whom my mercy will fail as long as he lives on this earth." [6]

St. Bridget relates that she saw the Mother of God begging graces of her Son in favor of a bandit who had retained some fear of the judgment of God: "Blessed be thou, beloved Mother," replied the Lord . . . . "Thy words have for me the savour of most delicious wine. They please me beyond all imagination . . . . Blessed be thy mouth, blessed be thy lips which utter words of mercy towards wretched sinners. Thou art justly called Mother of Mercy. Thou art so in truth: for thou dost not disclaim any misery and thou inclinest My heart to pity. Ask what Thou willest: neither thy charity nor thy requests shall be disappointed." [7]

"And so I believe," said Hugh of St. Victor, "that she exercises that office of mercy perpetually in heaven, in favor of the human race before the face of the Father and before her Son."

---

[6] *Revelations, Book IV,* chap. iv.
[7] *Revelations,* Book VI, ch. xxiii.

CHAPTER VII.

Our Lady Leads Us On To Perfection.

I. God Calls Us to Holiness.

II. Appeal to Mary's Motherhood.

III. Our Lady Unites Us with the Mysteries of Christ.

IV. Our Lady Unites Us with the Sacrifice of Christ.

    1. Our Lady's union with Christ's sacrifice.

    2. Our union with the sacrifice through the liturgy.

    3. Our union with the sacrifice in daily life.

V. To the Glory of the Holy Trinity.

    1. Our Lady unites us with the Father.

    2. Our Lady unites us with the Word.

    3. Our Lady unites us with the Holy Ghost.

Abandonment to Our Lady.

I. God Calls Us to Holiness.

God chose us in Christ "before the foundation of the world, that we should be holy and unspotted in His sight in charity. Who hath predestinated us unto the adoption of children through Jesus Christ unto Himself . . . unto the praise of the glory of His grace . . ." (Eph. i, 4-6).

That is our vocation. God calls us to share in His holiness by our adoption as sons in Christ. That is what St. Paul called the great mystery, "the dispensation of the mystery which hath been hidden from eternity in God" (Eph. iii, 9), the mystery of the total Christ.

We know by faith the secret of the inner life of God: the Father has a Son equal to Him; both are united in an embrace of infinite love whence the Holy Ghost proceeds . . . . The beatitude of the Father is to have a Son, "the brightness of His glory," says St. Paul (Heb. i, 3).

But now God extends His fatherhood: He shares His beatitude with His creatures, drawn out of nothing but lifted up to Him by His pure goodness: He makes them His children. He "hath translated us into the kingdom of the Son of His love" (Col. i, 13). That is the unimaginable grace of filial adoption: He adopts us in His beloved Son. From all eternity the Father looked with infinite satisfaction on the humanity united to the Word which would produce a rich flowering of holiness and love, not only in Christ the Redeemer, but in each of those that the Redeemer would unite with Himself: the Word incarnate leading His life of adoration and love in Himself and in His children by adoption. What astounding love! "Behold what manner of charity the Father hath bestowed upon us, that we should be called, and should be, the sons of God" (I John iii, 1).

In practice, holiness consists in becoming children of God through Christ: "whom He foreknew He also pre-destinated to be made conformable to the image of His Son" (Rom. viii, 29). The Word became incarnate, "that we might receive the adoption of sons" (Gal. iv, 5). He imparts the life of the Father to us and brings us into the divine family. Before our eyes He lived the life of a son; we must imitate Him. Our whole effort should be to unite with Jesus so as to share through Him in His filial life. There is no other means of going to God: "No man cometh to the Father but by Me" (John xiv, 6).

We must become sons of God in Jesus.

II. Appeal to Mary's Motherhood.

Since we have to become sons of God, let us appeal to Mary, Mother of the First-born. Her sovereign function is motherhood. She is daughter of the Father, Mother of the Word, Spouse of the Spirit: has she not every title for introducing us into the family of God? She is the queen of the kingdom of grace.

We ask her to extend her motherhood to us: she formed the Head of the mystical Christ, so may she deign to form His members. May she spread as widely as God desires the

Incarnation which began in her womb; may she watch over the growth of Christ's members as she watched over the growth of the Head; may she continue in us to be the mother of Christ.   She must now bring to the perfection of their life the children whom she conceived at the Incarnation and brought to birth on Calvary: bring each, as St. Paul says: "unto a perfect man, unto the measure of the age of the fulness of Christ" (Eph. iv, 13).   Our Lady can fulfil in us all that God wants of us.   Her motherhood corresponds to the fatherhood of God.   All our hopes of holiness rest in Mary's motherhood.   She possesses, and can give to us, that "fulness of God" of which St. Paul spoke (Eph. iii, 19). You may aspire to enter, like her, into the overshadowing power of the Father and the action of the Holy Ghost; and of you will be born the Holy One who will be called the Son of God.

III. Our Lady Unites Us with the Mysteries of Christ.

The historical duration of Christ's mysteries is over: their operation remains.   "Jesus Christ yesterday," says St. Paul, "and today and the same for ever" (Hebr. xiii, 8).   Why did He "love the Church and deliver Himself for it" (Gal. ii, 20)? In order to sanctify it. He did it during His earthly life by the mysteries of His humanity; He does it still by those same mysteries, which are realities always active and sanctifying.   They are an eternal reality.   "Their power never passes, nor will the love ever pass with which they were accomplished. The spirit, the state, the power, the merit, of the mystery is always present. The Spirit of God, for whom the mystery was performed; the inner state of the outward happening; the efficacity and the power which make the mystery alive and operative in us; that virtuous state and disposition, that merit by which He bought us for His Father and merited for us heaven, life, and Himself; even the actual delight, the eager disposition with which Jesus accomplished the mystery is still alive, actual, present to Jesus. So much so that if it were necessary, or pleasing to God His Father, He would be perfectly willing to suffer anew, and to accomplish anew the work, the action, the mystery. Therefore we must treat the things and the mysteries of Jesus not like things past and dead, but like things living and present and even eternal from which we have to gather precious eternal fruit." [1]

It is impossible to say how good it is for the soul to keep consciously united to the mysteries of Jesus, channels used by grace to give life to the world. That is the grace of the Rosary. The Rosary is Our Lady's means of uniting us to the ever-present mysteries of her Son, to the life-giving action of His humanity.

Is is easy for her to lead us into that blessed world of

---

[1] Cardinal Pierre de Bérulle, *Œuvres,* p. 1052.

the mysteries of Christ. They were accomplished in her presence; what is more, with her coöperation. She took an active part in them; they were events in her personal history at the same time as in her mission of motherhood. She grasped their marvellous economy and the connection of each with the sanctification of her children. She knows their fruitfulness because she always experienced it to the full. How can we conceive some idea of the union of Mary with Jesus in those mysteries? God worked an ineffable operation in her which makes one think of the inner life of the Trinity. "Jesus," says Bèrulle, "drew her into unity with Himself, and out of herself and her interior activity, so that she lived in Him; bearing up her holy aspirations by a kind of impression which was sweet, lofty, strong, and delightful, irresistibly drawing the Mother to the Son, the Virgin into Jesus." It was her whole life to contemplate the Word incarnate. "Mary's characteristic was to be intent on the inner spiritual life of her Son, to be pure capacity for Jesus, filled with Jesus." [2]

She leads us into that world of mysteries by faith. Vital contact with Christ is established by faith, which is the opening of our intelligence to the hidden riches of Christ; it is perfected in charity. Because the apostles believed in Jesus the Father loved them: "The Father Himself loveth

[2] *Ibid.*, pp. 497, 501.

you because you have believed that I came out from God"
(John xvi, 27). That faith draws down grace; Christ said:
"He that believeth in Me, as the Scripture saith, 'Out of his
belly shall flow rivers of living water' " (John vii, 38);
through it we attain to divine sonship.

Now, Our Lady is called *Virgo fidelis,* the Virgin of
faith, by the Church. Faith in the angel's word, though
he announced an unimaginable mystery, gave her entrance
into the mystery of Christ, that mystery which God, as St.
Paul says, had kept hidden from eternity. Those novel
secrets of the Trinity, the Incarnation, the Mystical Body,
how did Mary learn of them but from the word of God's
messenger? "Blessed art thou who has believed" (Luke i,
45), said her cousin to her. When she accepted the message
in faith she entered into the fulfilment of God's greatest
designs. The Word would live in her because of her faith.
All her love for her Son rested on that unshakeable faith
which God subjected to such terrible trials. Her pure
simple faith made her the handmaid of the Lord.

May Christ "dwell by faith in your hearts . . . rooted
and founded in charity" (Eph. iii, 17). That faith and
charity bind us to Christ and at last make ours the mysteries
that He lived for us. As St. Paul says: "God who is rich
in mercy, for His exceeding charity wherewith He loved us
. . . hath quickened us together in Christ . . . and hath

raised us up together, and hath made us sit together in the heavenly places, through Christ Jesus, that He might show in the ages to come the abundant riches of His grace in His bounty towards us in Christ Jesus" (Eph. ii, 4-7). We live again through all the mysteries of Jesus: nailed to the Cross with Him, buried with Him, risen along with Him.[3] By reliving the mysteries of Jesus, "we are made conformable to the image of the Son of God" (Rom. viii, 29).

"O Jesus, living in Mary, come and live in Thy servants, in the spirit of Thy holiness, in the fulness of Thy strength, in the perfection of Thy ways, in the truth of Thy virtues, in the communion of Thy mysteries victorious over every adverse power, in Thy Spirit, for the Glory of Thy Father." [4]

IV. Our Lady Unites Us with the Sacrifice of Christ.

1. OUR LADY'S UNION WITH CHRIST'S SACRIFICE.

Jesus lived with the Cross before His eyes. He ever walked towards Calvary. He was the Saviour of the world and the idea of His sacrifice never left Him for a moment. To understand His life one must look at it in the light of His death. From the moment of His entry into the world He said to God: "Sacrifice and oblation Thou wouldst not,

---

[3] St. Paul writes (Gal. ii, 19): "With Christ I am nailed to the cross;" and (Col. ii, 12): "Buried with Him in baptism, in whom also you are risen again by the faith of the operation of God."

[4] M. Olier.

but a body Thou hast fitted to Me . . . . Behold, I come"
(Heb. x, 5-7). That sacrifice, first offered in Mary's womb,
was to be continued for thirty-three years, until Jesus said:
"It is consummated" (John xix, 30).

And Our Lady? Like Jesus, she was dedicated to the
Cross. The grace of her divine motherhood as well as her
unique love required it. Because she was mother of God
she received a singular grace, exceeding by far all the gifts
received by the other children of adoption: a grace of
affinity, placing her, as Cajetan says, "within the confines
of divinity." In that Our Lady found her cross. She was
to resemble the Redeemer as closely as possible; the grace
of being foremost daughter of adoption modelled her on
Jesus, especially in His love of the cross. She was foremost
in cross-bearing, because she was foremost in grace.

And also because she was foremost in love. "When love
is boundless," says St. Albert the Great, "suffering is also
boundless." [5]

"There is no love comparable to Mary's," says Richard
of St. Lawrence, "and therefore no suffering equalled her
suffering." [6] Her martyrdom came from the excess of her
love.

Jesus gave her a share in His terrible secret. It was not

---

[5] St. Albert the Great, *Super missus,* q. 78.
[6] Richard of St. Lawrence, *In Cantica Canticorum,* ch. xxvi.

possible that Jesus should live in the cruel foresight of
Calvary and Mary, beside Him, lead a tranquil life. The
love between them demanded the closest union. It was
through love that Jesus gave Mary a share in his grievous
destiny. His sacrifice, His Passion, was the crowning-point
in His life: love required Him to lead His mother up to
it with Him. She was His mother: without a part in His
suffering, would she have been anything more than an
instrument?

Besides, if Jesus had not first offered Mary a share in
His sacrifice, Mary would have asked for it so humbly and
so ardently that her love would have obtained it. If she
longed to follow Jesus everywhere, she longed above all to
follow Him where He was to suffer. She wanted, in the
words of Jesus (Matt. xx, 22), to drink of His chalice. The
greatest gift of Jesus to Mary was her own Compassion, that
Compassion which enabled her to suffer with Him, to sacrifice herself with Him, to glorify God and to exercise her
motherhood of men. Was she not, moreover, the principle
of the Passion, as St. Augustine gives us to understand,
when she gave to her Son the nature which alone would
enable Him to suffer?

In order to understand the life of Our Lady we must
look at it, as we must look at the life of Jesus, in the light
of the Cross. Enlightened, from the moment of the In-

carnation, about the deep sense of the prophecies, and warned later by the venerable Simeon, she lived in the thought of the great sacrifice to come.　After the words of the holy man, she knew that she was going to live with a victim, in order to prepare Him for the sacrifice.　Thenceforward the Passion was always before her.　Everything reminded her of what had been foretold.　She herself said to St. Bridget: "Every time that I saw my Son, that I wrapped Him in swaddling clothes, that I looked at His hands and His feet, every time was my soul pierced as it were afresh by another sword of sorrow: I seemed to see Him already crucified." [7]　Our Lord revealed it to St. Teresa: "When thou seest My mother holding Me in her arms, do not imagine that her joys were unaccompanied by cruel torment: from the moment that she heard Simeon's words, My Father showed her by a vivid light what I should have to suffer." [8]　"What a prolonged martyrdom thou didst endure," says Rupert, "thou didst always foresee how thy Son would die." [9]　He puts the following words on Mary's lips: "Beware of limiting thy compassion for me to the hour that I saw my Son die.　Simeon's sword pierced me all my life.　When my Son was in my arms, when I suckled Him, I already saw His death.　What a

---

[7] *Revelations,* Book VI, ch. lvii.

[8] Edition of the Paris Carmelites, Vol. II, p. 247.

[9] Rupert, *In Cantica Canticorum,* Book III.

long-drawn out torture I endured!" [10]   "No, my sweet
Queen," said St. Anselm, "I do not believe that thou couldst
live for one single moment in the embrace of such sorrow
if the Spirit of life had not supported thee." [11]

When the day of the supreme sacrifice drew near, Our
Lady came to the Holy City.   She too might have said:
"I have a baptism wherewith I am to be baptized, and how
am I straitened until it be accomplished" (Luke xii, 50).
She knew that her Son's sacrifice would inaugurate the kingdom of God, that from His blood would be born sons of
God.   She knew that her Son was "the grain of wheat
falling into the ground" (of her womb), which, unless it
die, "itself remaineth alone, but if it die, it bringeth forth
much fruit" (John xii, 24, 25).   She saw all the predestined
who would be born of the sacrifice of Calvary, the multitude
of children of God born in the suffering of Calvary.   Her
love urged her.   When the day came, she was on Calvary.

Immense love drew her there.   She stood at the foot of
the Cross: stood in the face of suffering, because she dominated it.   In mind and heart she shared all her Son's tor-
ments.   She was wholly united and, as it were, identified
with Him, so intensely did she will with Him the same
will of God, so utterly did she follow it out to the end with

---

[10] Ibid.
[11] St. Anselm, *De excellent. Vir.*, ch. v.

absolute self-surrender. She sacrificed her Son for us. On Calvary above all she gave us Jesus. Like God the Father, she so loved us that she gave us her only Son.

2. OUR UNION WITH THE SACRIFICE THROUGH THE LITURGY.

It is absolutely necessary that we should unite with the sacrifice of Christ. That sacrifice, "the cause of eternal salvation" (Heb. v, 9) will only be fully efficacious if in mind, in heart, in our actions, we take an active part in it. Through union with the Passion we can fulfil our Christian vocation, for all graces come from the Cross. Jesus died to make us holy. "Christ loved the Church and delivered Himself up for it . . . . that He might present it to Himself a glorious Church, not having spot or wrinkle, or any such thing; but that it should be holy and without blemish" (Eph. v, 25-27).

Thus we understand why Our Lady brings us to the foot of the Cross: there flows the spring of holiness. Those who unite with Christ's oblation are sanctified: "For by one oblation He hath perfected for ever them that are sanctified" (Heb. x, 14).

We have two principal means of uniting with the Passion of Christ: the liturgy, and the acceptance of the sufferings of our daily life.

The altar perpetuates Calvary. In order that the graces of His death may be applied to all men in every age, Jesus unceasingly renews His sacrifice. He continues to be priest and victim.

At the communion He comes as priest. A priest's office is to adore and expiate. Within us He gives God perfect adoration, complete thanksgiving; He brings down pardon and divine grace. Within us, He adores, thanks, makes reparation, prays. All these acts of the eternal High Priest, which are done in us, become ours if we will. We may make our own all Christ's adoration, expiation, supplication. The interior movement which bore Jesus towards His Father can become the interior movement of our life. We can render the most perfect homage to God, as the liturgy says: "By Him and with Him and in Him be to Thee, Almighty Father, all honor and glory in the unity of the Holy Ghost."

Jesus comes also as a victim, in His state of immolation— He comes as sacrificial victim, with the holiness if we may put it so of the Christ-Victim. The sacrificial host is kept apart from every profane contact, reserved, consecrated to God. These are, according to St. Thomas, the marks of living holiness: freedom of affection from earthly things by purity and firm adhesion to God. The liturgy makes us share in the sublime holiness of Christ on the cross, where He was moved by pure love of His Father, where He was "an oblation and a sacrifice to God for an odor of sweetness" (Eph. v, 2).

What a source of grace for the Christian who truly takes part in the Mass! He pays to God the most perfect homage of filial adoration, he draws directly from the wellspring of all grace, he intensifies his inner life by contact with the death of Christ, little by little he becomes a living victim offered every day with the victim of Calvary. The Christian vocation is fulfilled.

But how could we take part in the sacrifice without remembering and invoking the Mother of the High Priest and of the Victim? Our Lady shared too intimately in her Son's priesthood during their earthly life not to be linked for ever with the exercise of that priesthood. As she was present on Calvary, she is present at Mass, which is a prolongation of Calvary. At the foot of the Cross, she stood by her Son as He offered Himself to the Father: at the altar she stands by the Church, as it offers itself with its Head renewing His sacrifice. Let us offer Jesus through Our Lady.

But Jesus does not want to be offered alone. The Mass is the sacrifice of Christ, but it is also the sacrifice of Christ's members, of the Church. It involves essentially the offering of Christ's members, immolated with Him in the same sacrifice, and in the same sentiments of self-abandonment and complete submission. When the priest offers the host to God, let Him also offer our soul, our body, our whole life, as St. Paul tells us to do: "I beseech you . . . that you present your bodies a living sacrifice, holy, pleasing unto God" (Rom. xii, 1).

Let this offering be made through Our Lady.

We must ask Mary to raise up servants formed in that liturgical spirit, who will be able, for the glory of God, to draw on the boundless resources of the liturgy, and more especially of the Mass. The value of the Mass is in itself boundless, but the servants of God have to use it, to appropriate it in their approach to God. In the first years of the Church, when Our Lady was still alive, she gave to the Masses celebrated by the apostles an efficacy of which we may judge by the vigorous growth of the Church in those blessed times. It is the saints who make the blood of Christ on our altars eloquent with His Father.

3. OUR UNION WITH THE SACRIFICE IN DAILY LIFE.

That union of thought, heart, and prayer with the sacrifice of Christ through the liturgy must be completed by the union with it of the actions of our daily life. St. Paul wrote to the Romans: "Know you not that all we who are baptized in Christ Jesus are baptized in His death? For we are buried together with Him by baptism into death (Rom. vi, 3, 4) . . . . Our old man is crucified with Him" (vi, 6). He said to the Galatians (ii, 19): "With Christ I am nailed to the Cross."

These words are exceptionally grave. They must guide our life. The grace of baptism has fashioned us after our Saviour, has made us participators in His death: a grace which is not isolated, but a seed that must germinate and fructify. Each Christian must reproduce the Passion, and, like St. Paul, be nailed to the Cross. "You also," since you are baptized, "reckon that you are dead to sin, but alive unto God in Christ Jesus our Lord" (Rom. vi, 11).

Christ Himself had warned us: "If any man will come after Me, let him deny himself and take up his cross daily" (Luke ix, 23).

Let us love the Cross in its various forms: trials, work, sickness, humiliations, and everything else; everything that Providence sends us, the sooner to make us resemble Christ. To these things we must add all the voluntary labor of mortification and penance, a baptismal engagement from which there is no dispensation.

When the hour comes of union with the sacrifice of Christ, nothing will help us more than to think of her who suffered so much for us. She suffered all her life. The law of sacrifice enveloped her. Her suffering itself grew constantly, for suffering and love grow side by side in predestined souls. She suffered in her body, but above all in her heart and soul. Hers was above all an interior martyrdom.

Days will come when physical pain grips us relentlessly. Then we must remember that we are members of Christ and that it is our vocation to continue His passion. Before us, Our Lady travelled by that royal road of the Cross. Think of her exile, her poverty, her loneliness. In whatever condition we are, even though it be extreme and beyond relief, we must ever see Our Lord and Our Lady bearing the same cross before us, and even heavier crosses.

Grief of heart is more terrible, but it is also more profitable. How searching are separations, mental torture, sadness even unto death! Then, above all, we must look at Mary. She suffered more in her heart than in her body. The intensity of her union with her Son increased her pain unimaginably. She would have suffered less had she loved less. She suffered alone. He who could have consoled her, the only one who understood her grief, Jesus, was precisely the principal cause of her agony. She had to suffer without sympathy, a terrible thing.

She teaches us to suffer for Jesus. "With Christ I am nailed to the Cross" (Gal. ii, 19), said St. Paul. It was far truer of Mary. She was associated with the work of redemption, and her motherhood made her enter into it more deeply than anyone. It is not enough to say that her sympathy made her feel the pain of her Son's sufferings: she entered into that pain, made it her own, identified herself with it. In truth there was only one Passion, endured at the same time by the Son and the Mother. Our Lady said it to St. Bridget: "In His Passion, His pain was my pain, because His heart was my heart." [12] As she had given her body at the Incarnation so that the Word could take our nature in her womb, unstintingly she gave her body, her heart, her soul, on Calvary, to endure the martyrdom that redeemed us. She suffered to establish the kingdom of God on earth. She was thinking of us. The mother was suffering: the mother of Jesus, but also the mother of His brethren, the mother of mercy, the advocate of sinners. One cannot discover the least motion of indignation in the Passion. Her Son delivered Himself up to God's justice, but invoked pardon for those who crucified Him. His mother did the same: her Son's executioners were also her children. Can you understand the fierce pain? The child of her virginal flesh, Jesus, put to death by those to whom, with ineffable love, she was giving birth in her heart!

"Forget not the groanings of thy mother" (Eccli. vii, 29),

---

[12] *Revelations*, Book VII, ch. xxxv.

Holy Scripture tells us. Our Lady wants to unite us with the Passion of her son. We were a part of that Passion. In the immolation of Christ we were not spectators, but agents, and in truth executioners. It was through our sins that Christ died and that Mary endured that dreadful martyrdom.

Our Lady desires us again in our day to have a share in the Passion, but through love now, and as St. Paul says, "to fill up those things that are wanting of the sufferings of Christ" (Col. i, 24). In our flesh we too must have our compassion for the sorrows of the Redeemer, compassion through the union of faith and love, through the action of penance and pain. That is the condition of our salvation: "heirs indeed of God and joint-heirs with Christ: yet so, if we suffer with Him" (Rom. viii, 17).

We must continue the redeeming work of Christ. The Church lives by His sacrifice. That sacrifice is renewed every day on the altar, but it is also continued in the suffering members of Jesus. The suffering of Christians is necessary for the salvation of the world: it is a source of life; it expiates, redeems, sanctifies.

When God does us the honor of calling us to suffer, let us be glad. Jesus gives Himself to us in all His mysteries but nowhere so much as in the mystery of the Cross. There are exchanges of love that take place in suffering:

it was on Calvary that Jesus gave His mother to John. "Unto you it is given for Christ, not only to believe in Him, but also to suffer for Him" (Phil. i, 29).

Our Lady teaches us to suffer in silence, hiddenly. Silence is the atmosphere of pain. There was silence on Calvary. We lose all that is most sanctifying in suffering by complaining, by talking of our troubles, by seeking consolation. Do not waste this precious grace.

Do you understand the union of the suffering soul with God? He who lives in the spirit of sacrifice does more than follow Jesus, he enters into the heart of His mystery. He can say with St. Paul: "I live, now not I, but Christ liveth in me" (Gal. ii, 20). Jesus said to Blessed Angela of Foligno: "Those who love and follow the way I followed, the way of sorrows, are My legitimate children. Those whose inner eye is fixed on My Passion and death, on My death which is the life and salvation of the world, on My death and not on other things, are my legitimate children. And the others are not." [13]

With the liturgy, let us ask Our Lady to give us that spirit of sacrifice, to be immolated with her Son:

> "Holy Mother, pierce me through,
> In my heart each wound renew
> Of my Saviour crucified."

---

[13] *Vie et révélations,* ch. xxxiii.

V. To the Glory of the Holy Trinity.

The essence of the inner life is devotion to the Holy Trinity. It is absolutely necessary to foster special sentiments of devotion for each of the Three Persons: filial love for the Father who gave us His only-begotten Son; entire and utter trust in the Word, our Redeemer and universal Mediator; self-surrender to the Holy Spirit dwelling in our souls, our guide, our master, our giver of gifts in the spiritual life.

Holiness is the inexpressible union of God with Himself in the Trinity of Persons. That infinite mutual clinging of Father and Son in the unity of the Holy Ghost, that movement of love consummating Their unity and crowning Their beatitude which causes God to find all His felicity in Himself, in His nature, and in the union of the Three Persons: that is the divine holiness. God is holy because the perfection of His nature separates Him infinitely from what is not Himself and because He is infinitely happy in the living embrace of the Three Persons together.

Similarly, Our Lady is holy. Her incommunicable name is *Sancta Maria*, Holy Mary, the holy virgin. She is holy because she is a virgin. Virginity is integrity, absence of division. She is holy because, being established in God at her creation, she never sought to cling to anything outside God, because she lived in God, entirely turned towards God.

For us holiness can only be imitation of that holiness of God: to cling to God with our intelligence, our will, and in our external actions so as to be, as St. Paul says, "one and the same spirit" (I Cor. xii, 11) with Him. Holiness means reducing all things to one, needing only God.

Who will lead us to that crowning-point of our life? Once more, Our Lady.

By her virginity she is the singularly beloved daughter of the Father: she will introduce us into the divine adoption, through her we shall become God's children.

By her divine motherhood, she is the mother of the only-begotten Son of God: she will make us brothers of her first-born.

By her human motherhood she is the bride of the Holy Ghost: through her we shall enter the Mystical Body, the graces of the Redemption will flow from her to us.

1. OUR LADY UNITES US WITH THE FATHER.

Mary is the supremely privileged daughter of the Father. God endowed Mary with all the beauty He could bring together in one creature. He willed the plenitude of nature and grace to meet in a creature who was only a creature, who would manifest the primal idea of God in creation: and He made the mother of His Son. She received more gifts than all angels and men together. God united and surpassed in the formation of the mother of His Son all the splendor that he had brought together in the angelic creation, all the life and power that He had bestowed in creating men. She, alone, is "full of grace." That says everything. In her you can read, more than in all other creatures, the power and love of God. She is the mirror of the Invisible, in as far as a creature can be.

The liturgy tells us that the purpose of the Incarnation was to bring us to the love of the invisible Father through the knowledge of the Son made visible in the flesh. God was not to remain in light inaccessible: He who is our life, our light, was to come within human reach. And so He manifested Himself first in the Word incarnate, and then in Mary: in Jesus, God in the midst of us; in Mary, the ideal form of the creature   ted with God. So we can see in Jesus what God is for us; in Mary what He wants us to be for Him.

This creation of Mary in the glory of virginity and grace already made her a singular object of the good pleasure of the Father. But their intimacy was unimaginably deepened when Our Lady gave birth to the Word. Here speech is powerless. "To establish an eternal alliance with thee," says Bossuet, "He willed thee to be the mother of His only-begotten Son, and Himself to be the Father of thine. O marvel! O abyss of charity! What mind would not be lost in consideration of the incomprehensible marks of His delight in Thee, from the moment that thou camest so near to Him through your common Son, the invisible bond of your holy alliance, the pledge of your mutual attachment so lovingly given by each to the other." "Our common Son!" God the Father and Mary meet in a common center of love, in Jesus their only-begotten Son; they say in ineffable union: "What is mine is thine." Only the union of the Three Divine Persons surpasses the union of the Father and the Blessed Virgin. "These two sacred persons, the Father who is in heaven and the mother who is on earth, are now bound together, and they too have as the bond of their holy union a divine Person, one Son, only-begotten, proceeding from them, who is between them the indissoluble bond to whom they are united for eternity." [14]

That union was to go still further: Our Lady's motherhood was to go as far as God's fatherhood of men. As she was mother of the Son by nature, so she became mother of the children of adoption. God has children, but it is through her: if grace gives children to the Father, does He not owe them to Our Lady? The Incarnation and Mary's fiat were necessary to form the Mystical Body of Christ.

---

[14] Cardinal Pierre de Bérulle.

The consequence of this is easy to guess: it is through Our Lady, our mother in grace, that we shall learn to act as sons of God.

Our whole supernatural life rests on the eternal sonship of the Word. Our sonship by adoption, St. Thomas tells us, is assimilation to the sonship of the eternal Word and makes us share in the unity of the Word with His Father. That is the basis of our supernatural state. But our actions must flow from that state: we must live, pray, work, suffer, as children of God. "Be ye therefore followers of God, as most dear children" (Eph. v, 1). "Walk . . . . as children of light" (John xii, 35, 36). "When you pray, say 'Father' " (Luke xi, 2).

The Father embraces with one embrace of love His only-begotten Son and His children of adoption: "He that loveth Me shall be loved by My Father . . . The Father Himself loveth you because you have loved Me and have believed that I came out from God" (John xiv, 21; xvi, 27). The eternal love of the Father for His Son flows down at the same time on His children of adoption, Jesus tells us: "Father . . . . the glory which Thou hast given Me I have given to them: that they may be one as We also are one: I in them, and Thou in Me: that they may be made perfect in one: and the world may know that Thou hast . . . . loved them as Thou hast loved Me" (John xvii, 22, 23).

The essential duty of the Christian therefore is to be in everything the child of God. Let us call on Mary's motherhood. Her sovereign mission is to form the children of God. The greatest happiness that we can give her is to let her bring us to the birth of grace. May she give us the sense of sonship, to love the Father and to speak to Him like children.

2. OUR LADY UNITES US WITH THE WORD.

Who could describe the union of Mary with Jesus? God alone can understand it. At the moment of the Incarnation, Mary gave the purest of her blood in the formation of the body of the Word. With what love she gave it! The Son of God responded by a love greater still: He gave her an immense grace, His divine life: He became wholly hers. With unique predilection the Trinity had formed the heart of the Blessed Virgin, that she might be the mother of the Word incarnate and love, fittingly, the Man-God. That union constantly increased during the earthly life of Jesus: think of the union springing from the life at Nazareth, work in common, poverty borne together, the same boundless desire for the salvation of men.

There were unimaginable exchanges: from Jesus to Mary flowed graces of light, an unbroken revelation so to say of the divine mysteries; from Mary to Jesus, perfect adaptation to those graces, admirable docility to every inspiration, the full flowering of love. Think above all of their union on Calvary, when a common will made them accept the astounding sacrifice.

"In speaking of thee, Mary, we speak of Jesus. Speaking of thy dispositions, we speak of those in which He was to be born. Thou art His, thou art through Him, thou art for Him. And as the divine Persons subsist in the Trinity only through their mutual relations, thou also, O holy Virgin, O person at once divine and human, divine by grace and human by nature, thou dost subsist in the being of grace only through thy relation to Jesus: thou didst live only by His grace before He lived to thee by nature. Thou breathest only by His Spirit, and thy graces and glories are His."[15]

We can understand that that ineffable union enables Our Lady to unite us with Jesus. That union with Jesus Christ is the goal that St. Paul continually sets for our spiritual life: "To me, to live is Christ" (Phil. i, 21).

Who will give us Christ? The Father. But He does it through Mary.

Our Lady reveals Jesus to us. She teaches us to contemplate Him. Did she not spend her whole life in that contemplation? We cannot think without a kind of inner

---

[15] Cardinal Pierre de Bérulle.

dazzlement of that interior life of Our Lady, looking at
Jesus with her mother-love and her boundless faith. The
actions of Jesus, His words, were every one of them like a
new revelation to Mary. Every motion of Jesus set up in
her a deep, inner vibration giving rise to acts of perfect
love.

The liturgy often invites us to ask Our Lady to reveal
her Son to us: "Show unto us the blessed fruit of thy womb,
Jesus." This knowledge of Jesus is indeed the starting-
point of love. The charity of Christ is then revealed to
us, the charity which made Him our brother.

"The charity of Christ presseth us" (II Cor. v, 14), as
the Apostle says. It urges us to live like Jesus, to suffer
like Jesus, to continue His work in the Church. What is
the whole Christian life but the continuation of the life of
Jesus by the practice of the same virtues? Christ extends
His life in me by grace. It is my life, but it is also His:
"I live, now not I, but Christ liveth in me" (Gal. ii, 20).
Glory is given to God: "All (things) are yours. And you
are Christ's and Christ is God's." (I Cor. iii, 22-23).

3. OUR LADY UNITES US WITH THE HOLY GHOST.

"The Holy Ghost will come upon thee," said the angel
to Our Lady. He had already come at her first sanctification, at the moment of Mary's creation, her Immaculate

Conception. "Hail, full of grace," said the angel also: every grace that a creature can receive she had already received to the full capacity of her being. Nothing was refused her of the gifts of God. The Trinity created a soul capable of receiving all Its gifts, in which It would find unique joy and a great object of glory. The Holy Spirit had so to say taken possession of Mary from the moment of her creation and had inundated her with divine life to prepare her to receive the Word. It was He who now made Mary fruitful. He formed in her the body of the Word: "The Holy Ghost shall come upon thee . . . and therefore also the Holy which shall be born of thee shall be called the Son of God" (Luke i, 35).

Since then it has been always so. The Holy Ghost continues to form the Mystical Body of Christ. He does it through Mary. The formation of the saints is their common work.

That tells us what the union of Our Lady with the Holy Ghost is. The Holy Ghost shows her the vocation of each of Christ's members, the degree of glory each is to obtain, his present dangers, the graces he needs. The whole plan of pre-destination is known to her: she fulfils it. Since no grace is given to any soul without Mary's mediation, it is a sign that the Holy Ghost reveals the condition of the Mystical Body to her and gives her the task of furthering its progress. What a union is this ever-present collaboration of the Holy Ghost and Our Lady in the formation of Christ! Together they produce Jesus in the Church. They produce Him in me. Wherever Jesus is born it is as it was the first time: He is born of the Holy Ghost and Mary.

Our Lady draws the Holy Ghost down into us: "When the Holy Ghost finds Mary in a soul," says St. Louis Mary Grignion de Montfort, "He flies thither, He enters fully, He communicates Himself abundantly to that soul in as far as it makes room for the spouse; and one of the great reasons why the Holy Spirit does not now work striking wonders in souls is that He does not find in them a close enough union with His faithful and indissoluble spouse."

By that active presence of the Holy Ghost, we complete our entrance into the divine family. He reveals Jesus to us as Jesus foretold. He gives us the sense of sonship. "You have received the spirit of adoption of sons whereby we cry: Abba, Father" (Rom. viii, 15). It is the Spirit of Jesus: "Because you are sons, God hath sent the Spirit of His Son into your hearts" (Gal. iv, 6). This spirit acts in us, directs our activity, as He directed the human activity of Jesus and as He directs the Church: "Whosoever are led by the Spirit of God, they are the sons of God," says St. Paul (Rom. viii, 14). So that we can pray like children: "The Spirit also helpeth our infirmity. For we know not what we should pray for as we ought; but the Spirit Himself asketh for us with unspeakable groanings" (Rom. viii, 26).

ABANDONMENT TO OUR LADY.

From these reflections let us conclude that we must abandon ourselves to Mary. We know her love for us. We know her power. She has light to guide us, goodness, grace. Let us trust ourselves to her, hope in her, accept the influence of her mother-love.

To abandon oneself means in the first place to give oneself to her. But it means more than that: it means to lay self aside, to forget oneself, to surrender oneself unreservedly. It is true that in the last resort it is to God that one is abandoning oneself, for His fatherly will alone governs the world, and especially the spiritual world. But we reach the perfection of abandonment to God by abandonment to Our Lady. Is she not closely associated with the government of the spiritual world? Her position as mother and queen is a real and active royalty. She forms the saints. God has conceived the idea of my spiritual life, of my life in Christ. He entrusts its realization to Our Lady: she holds the thread of all the events which Providence uses to make me a member of Christ, one of the elect. St. John tells us: "We have known and have believed the charity which God hath to us" (I John iv, 16);

then I have only to believe, to hope, to let myself be moulded.

Let us place in Mary's hands all that is ours, body and soul, sensibility, imagination, intelligence, free-will, merits. Let all these things be in her power. Let her direct our thoughts and desires, let her govern all our activity. Let us be really hers in order to be entirely God's.

Spiritual writers are wont to say that to practice this abandonment to Our Lady, the simplest way is to live with her, through her, and in her.

To live "with" Mary is easy when one loves her. By the intuitions of faith, we enter into communication with our mother and model. To pray, work, suffer, with her, changes life. It is association, continuous coöperation, with the Immaculate. Before us, she reached the perfection that we must reach. Wherever we go, however arduous our path, whatever cross we carry, let us look and we shall see Our Lady before us.

You who have the happiness of having served God for a long time, look at her: she too is the splendor of God, the revelation of the beauty of God. The nobility that the Lord wants to make conspicuous in Christ's members, the humility, purity, faith, charity, are living in the Blessed Virgin, so humble and so great, so loving and so strong.

And you, sinners, weak in faith, impure, proud: do you too live with her; she is so humanly pitiful, so sensitive to sorrow. However wretched you are, and because you are wretched, look at your mother.

She is always with us by her enveloping love; with us by the grace she distributes; with us by her prayer which is our strength; with us by her example which exhorts us; with us even when we do not think of her, for she is always thinking of us, as a mother of her children, in joy and sorrow, "now and at the hour of our death," as every day we ask her to think of us. It is a companionship of influence and love. We can say with Elizabeth: "Whence is this to me that the mother of my Lord should come to me?"

We must live "through" Our Lady: she is our Mediatrix, *Janua coeli,* gate of heaven, gate of grace. Through her, Christ comes to us, through her we go to Christ. She helps our prayer. She tempers what in the Godhead might crush us. She is the "mirror of justice," and of divine holiness, she makes the divine perfection more accessible. Hope of holiness and of heaven becomes easier for us through her. She supplies by her Son's merits and her own what was wanting in our actions and petitions. We offer our prayers and our work through her. It seems as if she said to us, like her Son, "I pray for them" (John xvii, 9). Rising from a heart that lacks fervor, our poor prayer has the good fortune to meet Mary's prayer, which takes hold of it, wraps it in love, and makes it hers: it becomes the prayer of mother and children and goes up to the throne of God.

To live through Mary is to forget self, to be detached from self. One of the principal obstacles to the spiritual life is that preoccupation with self which makes us forget God's views, which prevents us from clearly seeing into the designs of Providence. To renounce our own conceits and adapt ourselves to Our Lady's views, is to enter into the accomplishment of the divine designs. For that is needed interior silence which makes us attentive, humility of mind which makes us docile and flexible to God's leading. It is impossible to express how rapidly those souls advance, whom self-forgetfulness makes docile to Our Lady's impulsion; or to describe the inner peace they enjoy. Abandonment to Our Lady has delivered them from their own judgment in the direction of their life, and therefore from the illusions of sensibility and pride. Now Our Lady gently and strongly directs their efforts, their prayers, their thoughts. She is truly the Queen who reigns with motherly but powerful majesty. The soul enters deeply into the intimacy of God.

To live "in" Mary, under her constant influence, in dependence on her and, as it were, clinging to her, having "the same heart and mind"; to make her intentions ours; to pray like her in the same spirit of humility and adoration, to unite with her religious reverence, her love: to become, as St. Louis Mary Grignion de Montfort says, "living copies of Mary": it is a great gift to reach that intimacy with the Mother of God. It is the most direct means of living in Christ. It is in Our Lady that we shall find the life of Christ ready to be shared with us. "I implore you," said M. Olier, "to withdraw often into the divine inner life of Mary whom God set up as mediatrix of the sacred gift of His Son to the Church. In that sanctuary you will find movements of adoration, praise, and love of God a thousand times more august than any that will ever be offered Him by creation . . . . For that reason I continue to implore you to go to that divine sanctuary, because in union with the Blessed Virgin you will make more progress for God and for the Church and for yourselves, than by any other practices that you could adopt."

"O holy Virgin, Mother of God, Queen of men and of angels, marvel of heaven and of earth, I revere thee in every way that I can according to God; I revere thee as I ought according to thy greatness, and as the only-begotten Son, Jesus Christ Our Lord, wishes thee to be revered on earth and in heaven.

"I offer thee my soul and my life; and I desire to belong to thee for ever, and to pay thee some special homage and mark of dependence in time and eternity. Mother of grace and mercy, I choose thee for the mother of my soul, in honor of God's good pleasure in choosing thee for His Mother. Queen of men and of angels, I accept and acknowledge thee for my sovereign in honor of the dependence on thee as His Mother in which the Son of God, my Saviour and my God, willed to live; and in that capacity I give thee all the power over my soul and my life that according to God I can give. O holy Virgin, look on me as thy thing, and through thy goodness treat me as the subject of thy sway, and the object of thy mercies.

"O Source of life and grace, refuge of sinners, I have recourse to thee to be delivered from sin, to be preserved from eternal death. May I be under thy guardianship, may I have a share in thy privileges, and may I obtain by thy glories and privileges and by the right of belonging to thee, what because of my offences I do not deserve; may the last hour of my life, which will decide my eternity, be in thy hands, in honor of that happy moment of the Incarnation when God became Man and made thee Mother of God.

"O thou who art both Virgin and Mother! O sacred Temple of the Divinity! O marvel of heaven and of earth! O Mother of my God! I am thine by the general right and title of thy greatness, but I wish to be thine also by the special right of my choice and my free will. I give myself to thee and to thy only-begotten Son, Jesus Christ Our Lord;

and I wish to pass no day without giving Him and thee some special homage and marks of my dependence and servitude, in which I desire to die and to live for ever." [16]

---

[16] Prayer of Cardinal Pierre de Bérulle.